Jules Verne

Meridiana

The Adventures of Three Englishmen and Three Russians in South Africa

Jules Verne

Meridiana

The Adventures of Three Englishmen and Three Russians in South Africa

ISBN/EAN: 9783744752718

Printed in Europe, USA, Canada, Australia, Japan

Cover: Foto ©ninafisch / pixelio.de

More available books at **www.hansebooks.com**

ADVENTURES OF THREE ENGLISHMEN AND THREE RUSSIANS IN SOUTH AFRICA.

MERIDIANA:

THE ADVENTURES

OF

THREE ENGLISHMEN AND THREE RUSSIANS

IN

SOUTH AFRICA.

BY

JULES VERNE.

Translated from the French.   With numerous Illustrations.

NEW YORK:
SCRIBNER, ARMSTRONG & CO.,
654 BROADWAY.
1874.

Works of Jules Verne,
PUBLISHED BY
SCRIBNER, ARMSTRONG & CO.

THE COMPLETE AND AUTHORIZED EDITIONS.

CAUTION.

The public are cautioned against any editions of the works named below which do not bear the imprint of SCRIBNER, ARMSTRONG & CO. Any edition of these particular works published under other imprints are PIRATED, and cannot fail to be *inferior in every particular.* Editions bearing our imprint are issued under a direct arrangement with the French and English publishers of JULES VERNE, and are *authorized in text and complete in illustration.*

MERIDIANA:

THE ADVENTURES OF THREE ENGLISHMEN AND THREE RUSSIANS IN SOUTH AFRICA. By JULES VERNE. Translated from the French. With 48 illustrations. One vol. 12mo, cloth, gilt side and back. Price, 75 cents. The only edition authorized in text and complete in illustrations.

FROM THE EARTH TO THE MOON

IN 97 HOURS AND 20 MINUTES AND A TRIP AROUND IT. Eighty full-page illustrations, beautifully bound in cloth, black and gilt. Price, $3.00.

A JOURNEY to the CENTRE of the EARTH.

Translated from the French of JULES VERNE, author of *"From the Earth to the Moon Direct," "The Mysterious Island,"* &c., &c. With fifty-two illustrations by Riou.

Popular edition, 20 illustrations, 75c. *Complete edition,* 53 illustrations, on super-calendered paper, handsomely bound in cloth, black and gilt, beveled boards, $3.00.

SCRIBNER, ARMSTRONG & CO.,

654 BROADWAY, NEW YORK

CONTENTS.

CHAPTER I.
ON THE BANKS OF THE ORANGE RIVER . . . . 1 (PAGE)

CHAPTER II.
OFFICIAL PRESENTATIONS 13

CHAPTER III.
THE LAND JOURNEY 21

CHAPTER IV.
A FEW WORDS ABOUT THE "METRE" 31

CHAPTER V.
A HOTTENTOT VILLAGE 39

CHAPTER VI.
BETTER ACQUAINTANCE 49

CHAPTER VII.
THE BASE OF THE TRIANGLE 59

CHAPTER VIII.
THE TWENTY-FOURTH MERIDIAN 69

CONTENTS.

CHAPTER IX.
The Kraal 76

CHAPTER X.
The Rapid 89

CHAPTER XI.
A Missing Companion 96

CHAPTER XII.
A Station to Sir John's liking 106

CHAPTER XIII.
Pacification by Fire 117

CHAPTER XIV.
A Declaration of War 127

CHAPTER XV.
A Geometric Progression 136

CHAPTER XVI.
Danger in Disguise 146

CHAPTER XVII.
An Unexpected Blight 154

CHAPTER XVIII.
The Desert 167

CHAPTER XIX.
Science Undaunted 179

CONTENTS.

CHAPTER XX.

	PAGE
STANDING A SIEGE	189

CHAPTER XXI.

SUSPENSE	200

CHAPTER XXII.

HIDE AND SEEK	211

CHAPTER XXIII.

HOMEWARD BOUND	225

LIST OF ILLUSTRATIONS.

	PAGE
FRONTISPIECE.	
William Emery and the Bushman	8
At length an exclamation of the Bushman made his heart beat	18
Meeting of Members of the Exped·tion	20
"The Hunter Mokoum," said William Emery, presenting his Companion	24
All these Objects were deposited on the Beach	26
The Mission Home Establishment	44
Chief Moulibahan	46
William Emery and Michael Zorn in advance of the Expedition	53
The Bushman pointing to the Plain	58
Commencement of the Geodesic Operations	61
Measuring the Arc of the Meridian	69
Taking the Measurements	69
The Astronomers at Work	72
Encampment under an immense Baobab	74
The Hunters	80
The Elephant and the Dog	86
"He is ours! he is ours!"	87
The Hippopotamus did not quit his hold, but shook the Boat as a Dog would a Hare	95
"There he is," cried Mokoum	103
A missing Companion	104
It was a deep Grotto, strewn with Bones and stained with Blood	112
The Entrance to the Lion's Den	112
A Ball from the Bushman arrested the Lioness	115
"Well," said Mokoum, "I hope you like our African Partridges"	116

LIST OF ILLUSTRATIONS.

	PAGE
Sir John was soon asleep	124
The Forest on Fire	125
"War is declared between England and Russia"	133
The Parting of Emery and Zorn	135
"The Rhinoceros!" exclaimed Sir John	141
The Advance of the Caravan	148
The Hunters glided through the Creepers and Brushwood	151
The empty Oryx Skin	152
Emery and two Natives struck by Lightning	158
A strange Cloud	161
Crossing the Desert	169
"The Ngami! the Ngami!"	172
The English come to the relief of the Russians	178
On Guard on Mount Scorzef	189
An Attack on Mount Scorzef	193
The Rice of the Bochjesmen	196
Watching for the Signal from Mount Volquiria	204
The Steamboat leaving Mount Scorzef	210
Palander robbed by the Chacma	217
Palander's Combat with the Chacma	224
Descending the Zambesi	229
Adieu to Mokoum	230
The Natives regarded with superstitious admiration the smoking vessel	230

MERIDIANA;

THE ADVENTURES OF THREE ENGLISHMEN AND THREE RUSSIANS.

CHAPTER I.

ON THE BANKS OF THE ORANGE RIVER.

ON the 27th of January, 1854, two men lay stretched at the foot of an immense weeping willow, chatting, and at the same time watching most attentively the waters of the Orange River. This river, the Groote of the Dutch, and the Gariep of the Hottentots, may well vie with the other three great arteries of Africa—the Nile, the Niger, and the Zambesi. Like those, it has its periodical risings, its rapids and cataracts. Travellers whose names are known over part of its course, Thompson, Alexander, and Burchell, have each in their turn praised the clearness of its waters, and the beauty of its shores.

At this point the river, as it approached the Duke of

York Mountains, offered a magnificent spectacle to the view. Insurmountable rocks, imposing masses of stone, and trunks of trees that had become mineralized by the action of the weather, deep caverns, impenetrable forests, not yet disturbed by the settler's axe, all these, shut in by a background formed by the mountains of the Gariep, made up a scene matchless in its magnificence. There, too, the waters of the river, on account of the extreme narrowness of their bed, and the sudden falling away of the soil, rushed down from a height of 400 feet. Above the fall there were only surging sheets of water, broken here and there by points of rock wreathed with green boughs; below, there was only a dark whirlpool of tumultuous waters, crowned with a thick cloud of damp vapour, and striped with all the colours of the rainbow. From this gulf there arose a deafening roar, increased and varied by the echoes of the valley.

Of these two men, who had evidently been brought into this part of South Africa by the chances of an exploration, one lent only a vague attention to the beauties of nature that were opened to his view. This indifferent traveller was a hunting bushman, a fine type of that brave, bright-eyed, rapidly-gesticulating race of men, who lead a wandering life in the woods. Bushman, a word derived from the Dutch " Bochjesman," is literally "a man of the bushes," and is applied to the wandering tribes that scour the country in the N.W. of Cape Colony. Not a family of these bushmen is sedentary; they pass their lives in roaming over the region lying between the Orange River and the mountains of the East, in pillaging farms, and in destroying the crops of the overbearing colonists, by whom they have been driven back towards the interior of the country, where more rocks than plants abound.

This bushman, a man of about forty years of age, was very tall, and evidently possessed great muscular strength, for even when at rest his body presented the attitude of action. The clearness, ease, and freedom of his movements stamped him as an energetic character, a man cast in the same mould as the celebrated "Leather-stocking," the hero of the Canadian prairies, though perhaps possessing less calmness than Cooper's favourite hunter, as could be seen by the transient deepening of colour in his face, whenever he was animated by any unusual emotion.

The bushman was no longer a savage like the rest of his race, the ancient Laquas; for, born of an English father and a Hottentot mother, the half-breed, through his association with strangers, had gained more than he had lost, and spoke the paternal tongue fluently. His costume, half-Hottentot, half-European, consisted of a red flannel shirt, a loose coat and breeches of antelope hide, and leggings made of the skin of a wild cat; from his neck hung a little bag containing a knife, a pipe, and some tobacco; he wore on his head a kind of skull-cap of sheep-skin; a belt, made from the thick thong of some wild animal, encircled his waist; and on his naked wrists were rings of ivory, wrought with remarkable skill. From his shoulders flowed a "kross," a kind of hanging mantle, cut out of a tiger's skin, and falling as low as the knees. A dog of native breed was sleeping near him, while he himself was smoking a bone pipe in quick puffs, giving unequivocal signs of impatience.

"Come, let's be calm, Mokoum," said his interlocutor. "You are truly the most impatient of mortals whenever you are not hunting; but do understand, my worthy companion, that we can't change what is. Those whom we are expecting will come sooner or later—to-morrow, if not to-day."

The bushman's companion was a young man, from twenty-five to twenty-six years of age, and quite a contrast to him. His calm temperament was shown in every action; and it could be decided without a moment's hesitation that he was an Englishman. His much too homely costume proved him to be unaccustomed to travelling. He gave one the idea of a clerk who had wandered into a savage country, and one looked involuntarily to see if he carried a pen behind his ear, like a cashier, clerk, accountant, or some other variety of the great family of the bureaucracy.

In truth, this young man was not a traveller, but a

distinguished *savant*, William Emery, an astronomer attached to the Observatory at the Cape—a useful establishment, which has for a long time rendered true services to science.

The scholar, rather out of his element, perhaps, in this uninhabited region of South Africa, several hundred miles from Cape Town, could hardly manage to curb the impatience of his companion.

"Mr. Emery," replied the hunter in good English, "here we have been for eight days at the place appointed on the Orange, the cataract of Morgheda. It is indeed a long time since it has befallen a member of my family to remain eight days in one place: you forget that we are rovers, and that our feet burn at lingering here."

"My friend Mokoum," replied the astronomer, "those we are waiting for are coming from England, and surely we can allow them eight days of grace: we must take into account the length of the passage, and the hindrances which a steam-vessel must meet with in ascending the Orange; and, in short, the thousand difficulties belonging to such an undertaking. We have been told to make every preparation for a journey of exploration in South Africa, and that being done, to come here to the Falls of Morgheda and wait for my colleague, Colonel Everest, of the Cambridge Observatory. Well, here are the Falls of Morgheda, we are at the place appointed, and we are waiting: what more do you want, my worthy bushman?"

The hunter doubtless did want more, for his fingers played feverishly with the lock of his rifle, an excellent Manton, a weapon of precision with conical shot, and which could bring down a wild cat or an antelope at a distance of eight or nine hundred yards. Thus it may be seen that the bushman had put aside the quiver of aloes and the poisoned darts of his fellow-countrymen for the use of European weapons.

"But are you not mistaken, Mr. Emery?" replied Mokoum. "Is it really at the Falls of Morgheda, and towards the end of this month of January, that they have appointed to meet you?"

"Yes, my friend," quietly answered William Emery, "and here is the letter from Mr. Airy, the director of the Greenwich Observatory, which will show you that I am not mistaken."

The bushman took the letter that his companion gave him. He turned it over and over like a man not very familiar with the mysteries of penmanship; then giving it back to William Emery, he said, "Tell me again what the blotted piece of paper says."

The young astronomer, endowed with a patience proof against every thing, began again, for the twentieth time, the story he had so often told to his friend the hunter At the end of the foregoing year, William Emery had received a letter telling him of the approaching arrival of Colonel Everest, and an international scientific commission in Southern Africa. What the plans of the commission were, and why it came to the extremity of the continent of Africa, Emery could not say, Mr. Airy's letter being silent on that point; but following the instructions that he had received, he hastened to Lattakoo, one of the most northern stations in the Hottentot country, to prepare waggons, provisions, and, in short, every thing that could be wanted for the victualling of a Bochjesman caravan. Then, as he knew the reputation of the native hunter, Mokoum, who had accompanied Anderson in his hunting expeditions in Western Africa, and the intrepid David Livingstone on his first journey of exploration to Lake Ngami and the falls of the Zambesi, he offered him the command of this same caravan.

This done, it was arranged that the bushman, who knew the country perfectly, should lead William Emery along the banks of the Orange to the Morgheda Falls, the place appointed for the scientific commission to join them. This commission was to take its passage in the British frigate "Augusta," to reach the mouth of the Orange on the western coast of Africa, as high as Cape Voltas, and to ascend the river as far as the cataracts. William Emery and Mokoum had therefore brought a waggon, which they had left at the bottom of the valley, to carry the strangers and their baggage to Lattakoo, unless they preferred getting there by the Orange and its affluents, after they had avoided the Falls of Morgheda by a land journey of some miles.

This story ended, and at length really impressed on the bushman's mind, he advanced to the edge of the gulf to whose bottom the foaming river threw itself with a crash: the astronomer followed, for there a projecting point commanded a view of the river, below the cataract, for a distance of several miles. For some minutes Mokoum and his companion gazed attentively at the part of the river where it resumed its tranquillity about a quarter of a mile below them, but not an object, either boat or pirogue, disturbed its course. It was then three o'clock. The month of January here corresponds to the July of northern countries, and the sun, almost vertical in lat. $29°$, heated the atmosphere till the thermometer stood at $105°$ Fahrenheit in the shade. If it had not been for the westerly breeze, which moderated the heat a little, the temperature would have been unbearable for any but a bushman. Still, the young astronomer, with his cool temperament, all bone and all nerves, did not feel it too much: the thick foliage of the trees which overhung the abyss protected him from the direct attacks of the sun's rays. Not a bird enlivened the solitude during these hot hours of the day; not an animal

William Emery and the Bushman.—[Page 8.]

left the cool shade of the bushes to trust itself along the glades; not a sound would have been heard in this deserted region, even if the cataract had not filled the whole air with its roar.

After gazing for ten minutes, Mokoum turned to William Emery, stamping impatiently with his large foot; his penetrating eyes had discovered nothing.

"Supposing your people don't come?" he asked the astronomer.

"They'll come, my brave hunter," answered William Emery: "they are men of their word, and punctual, like all astronomers. Besides, what fault do you find with them? The letter says they are to arrive at the end of January; this is the 27th, and these gentlemen have still a right to four more days before they need to reach the Morgheda Falls."

"And supposing they have not come at the end of those four days?" asked the bushman.

"Well! then, master hunter, there will be a chance for us to show our patience, for we will wait for them until I have certain proof that they are not coming at all."

"By our god Ko!" cried the bushman in a sonorous voice, "you are a man who would wait until the Gariep had emptied all its roaring waters into that abyss!"

"No, hunter, no," replied Emery in his ever quiet tone; "but we must let reason govern our actions; and what does reason tell us? This:—that if Colonel Everest and his companions, wearied with a tiresome journey, in want perhaps, and lost in this lonely country, were not to find us at the place of rendezvous, we should be to blame in every way. If any thing went wrong, the responsibility would rest on us; we ought, therefore, to stay at our post as long as it is our duty to do so. And besides, we want for nothing here: our waggon is waiting for us at the bottom of the valley, and gives us shelter at night; we have plenty of provisions; nature here is magnificent and worthy of our admiration; and it is quite a new pleasure to me to spend a few days in these splendid forests on the banks of this matchless river. As for you, Mokoum, what can you want more? Game, both hairy and feathered, abounds in the forests, and your rifle keeps us supplied with venison. Hunt, my brave hunter! kill time by killing deer and buffaloes! Go, my good bushman; I'll watch for the loiterers meanwhile, and *your* feet, at any rate, will run no risk of taking root."

The hunter thought the astronomer's advice was good, and decided that he would go for a few hours and beat the neighbouring bushes and brushwood. Lions, hyenas, and leopards would not disturb such a Nimrod as he, so well accustomed to the African forests. He whistled to his dog Top, an animal of the hyena breed from the desert of Kalahari, and a descendant of that race of which the Balabas formerly made pointers. The intelligent creature, as impatient, seemingly, as his master, bounded up, and showed by his joyous barking how much he was gratified at the bushman's intention. Soon both man and dog disappeared among the thick masses of wood which crowned the background of the cataract. William Emery, now alone, again stretched himself at the foot of the willow, and while he was waiting for the heat to send him to sleep, began to think over his actual position. Here he was, far away from any inhabited spot, on the banks of the Orange river, a river as yet but little explored. He was waiting for Europeans, fellow-countrymen who had left their homes to run the risks of a distant expedition. But what was the expedition for? What scientific problem could it want to solve in the deserts of South Africa? What observation could it be trying to take in lat. 30° S.? That was just what Mr. Airy, the director of the Greenwich Observatory, did not tell in his letter. As for Emery himself, they asked for his co-operation as for that of a scientific man who was familiar with the climate of those southern latitudes, and as he was openly engaged in scientific labours, he was quite at the disposal of his colleagues in the United Kingdom.

As the young astronomer lay musing over all these things, and asking himself a thousand questions which he could not answer, his eyelids became heavy, and at length he slept soundly. When he awoke, the sun was already hidden behind the western hills, whose picturesque outline stood out sharply against the bright horizon. Some gnawings of hunger told him that supper-time was near; it was, in fact, six o'clock, and just the hour for returning to the waggon at the bottom of the valley. At that very moment a report resounded from a grove of arborescent heaths, from twelve to fifteen feet high, which was growing along the slope of the hills on the right. Almost immediately the bushman and Top made their appearance at the edge of the wood, the former dragging behind him the animal that he had just shot. "Come, come, master purveyor!" cried Emery, "what have you got for supper?"

"A springbok, Mr. William," replied the hunter, throwing down an animal with horns curved like a lyre. It was a kind of antelope, more generally known by the name of "leaping buck," and which is to be met with in every part of South Africa. It is a charming animal, with its cinnamon-coloured back, and its croup covered with tufts of silky hair of a dazzling whiteness, whilst its under part is in shades of chestnut brown; its flesh, always excellent eating, was on this occasion to form the evening repast.

The hunter and the astronomer, lifting the beast by means of a pole placed across their shoulders, now left the head of the cataract, and in half an hour reached their encampment in a narrow gorge of the valley, where the waggon, guarded by two Bochjesman drivers, was waiting for them.

CHAPTER II.

OFFICIAL PRESENTATIONS.

FOR the next three days, the 28th, 29th, and 30th of January, Mokoum and William Emery never left the place of rendezvous. While the bushman, carried away by his hunting instincts, pursued the game and deer in the wooded district lying near the cataract, the young astronomer watched the river. The sight of this grand, wild nature enchanted him, and filled his soul with new emotions. Accustomed as he was to bend over his figures and catalogues day and night, hardly ever leaving the eye-piece of his telescope, watching the passage of stars across the meridian and their occultations, he delighted in the open-air life in the almost impenetrable woods which covered the slope of the hills, and on the lonely peaks that were sprinkled by the spray from the Morgheda as with a damp dust. It was joy to him to take in the poetry of these vast solitudes, and to refresh his mind, so wearied with his mathematical speculations; and so he beguiled the tediousness of his waiting, and became a new man, both in mind and body. Thus did the novelty of his situation explain his unvarying patience, which the bushman could not share in the least; so there were continually on the part of Mokoum the same recriminations, and on the part of Emery the same quiet answers, which, however, did not quiet the nervous hunter in the smallest degree.

And now the 31st of January had come, the last day fixed in Airy's letter. If the expected party did not then arrive, Emery would be in a very embarrassing position; the delay might be indefinitely prolonged. How long, then, ought he to wait?

"Mr. William," said the hunter, "why shouldn't we go to meet these strangers? We cannot miss them; there is only one road, that by the river, and if they are coming up, as your bit of paper says they are, we are sure to meet them."

"That is a capital idea of yours, Mokoum," replied the astronomer: "we will go on and look out below the falls. We can get back to the encampment by the side valleys in the south. But tell me, my good bushman, you know nearly the whole course of the river, do you not?"

"Yes, sir," answered the hunter, "I have ascended it twice from Cape Voltas to its juncture with the Hart on the frontier of the Transvaal Republic."

"And it is navigable all the way, except at the Falls of Morgheda?"

"Just so, sir," replied the bushman. "But I should add that at the end of the dry season the Orange has not much water till within five or six miles of its mouth; there is then a bar, where the swell from the west breaks very violently."

"That doesn't matter," answered the astronomer, "because at the time that our friends want to land it will be all right. There is nothing then to keep them back, so they will come."

The bushman said nothing, but shouldering his gun, and whistling to Top, he led the way down the narrow path which met the river again 400 feet lower.

It was then nine o'clock in the morning, and the two explorers (for such they might truly be called) followed the river by its left bank. Their way did not offer the smooth and easy surface of an embankment or towing-path, for the river-banks were covered with brushwood, and quite hidden in a bower of every variety of plants; and the festoons of the "cynauchum filiform," mentioned by Burchell, hanging from tree to tree, formed quite a network of verdure in their path; the bushman's knife, however, did not long remain inactive, and he cut down the obstructive branches without mercy. William Emery drank in the fragrant air, here especially impregnated with the camphor-like odour of the countless blooms of the diosma. Happily there were sometimes more open places along the bank devoid of vegetation, where the river flowed quietly, and abounded in fish, and these enabled the hunter and his companion to make better progress westward, so that by eleven o'clock they had gone about four miles. The wind being in the west, the roar of the cataract could not be heard at that distance, but on the other hand, all sounds below the falls were very distinct. William Emery and the hunter, as they stood, could see straight down the river for three or four miles. Chalk cliffs, 200 feet high, overhung and shut in its bed on either side.

"Let us stop and rest here," said the astronomer; "I haven't your hunter's legs, Mokoum, and am more used to the starry paths of the heavens than to those on terra firma; so let us have a rest; we can see three or four miles down the river from here, and if the steamer should turn that last bend we are sure to see it."

The young astronomer seated himself against a giant euphorbia, forty feet high, and in that position looked down the river, while the hunter, little used to sitting, continued to walk along the bank, and Top roused up clouds of wild birds, to which, however, his master gave no heed. They had been here about half an hour, when William Emery noticed that Mokoum, who was standing about 100 feet below him, gave signs of a closer attention. Was it likely that he had seen the long-expected boat? The astronomer, leaving his mossy couch, started for the spot where the hunter stood, and came up to him in a very few moments.

"Do you see any thing, Mokoum?" he asked.

"I *see* nothing, Mr. William," answered the bushman, "but it seems to me that there is an unusual murmur down the river, different to the natural sounds that are so familiar to my ears." And then, telling his companion to be quiet, he lay down with his ear on the ground, and listened attentively. In a few minutes he got up, and shaking his head, said,—

"I was mistaken; the noise I thought I heard was nothing but the breeze among the leaves or the murmur of the water over the stones at the edge; and yet——"

The hunter listened again, but again heard nothing.

"Mokoum," then said Mr. William Emery, "if the noise you thought you heard is caused by the machinery of a steamboat, you would hear better by stooping to the level of the river; water always conducts sound more clearly and quickly than air."

"You are right, Mr. William," answered Mokoum, "for more than once I have found out the passage of a hippopotamus across the river in that way."

The bushman went nimbly down the bank, clinging to the creepers and tufts of grass on his way. When he got to the level of the river, he went in to his knees, and stooping down, laid his ear close to the water.

"Yes!" he exclaimed, in a few minutes, "I was not mistaken; there is a sound, some miles down, as if the waters were being violently beaten; it is a continual monotonous splashing which is introduced into the current."

"Is it like a screw?" asked the astronomer.

"Perhaps it is, Mr. Emery; they are not far off."

William Emery did not hesitate to believe his companion's assertion, for he knew that the hunter was endowed with great delicacy of sense, whether he used his eyes, nose, or ears. Mokoum climbed up the bank again, and they determined to wait in that place, as they could easily see down the river from there. Half an hour passed, which to Emery, in spite of his calmness, appeared interminable. Ever so many times he fancied he saw the dim outline of a boat gliding along the water, but he was always mistaken. At last an exclamation from the bushman made his heart leap.

"Smoke!" cried Mokoum.

Looking in the direction indicated by the bushman, Emery could just see a light streak rolling round the bend of the river: there was no longer any doubt. The vessel advanced rapidly, and he could soon make out the funnel pouring forth a torrent of black smoke mingling with white steam. They had evidently made up their fires to increase their speed, so as to reach the appointed place on the exact day. The vessel was still about seven miles from the Falls

At length an exclamation of the Bushman made his heart beat.—[Page 18.]

of Morgheda. It was then twelve o'clock, and as it was not a good place for landing, the astronomer determined to return to the foot of the cataract: he told his plan to the hunter, who only answered by turning back along the path he had just cleared along the left bank of the stream. Emery followed, and, turning round for the last time at a bend in the river, saw the British flag floating from the stern of the vessel. The return to the falls was soon effected, and in an hour's time the bushman and the astronomer halted a quarter of a mile below the cataract; for there the shore, hollowed into a semicircle, formed a little creek, and as the water was deep right up to the bank, the steamboat could easily land its passengers. The vessel could not be far off now, and it had certainly gained on the two pedestrians, although they had walked so fast; it was not yet in sight, for the lofty trees which hung quite over the river-banks into the water, and the slope of the banks themselves, did not allow of an extensive view. But although they could not hear the sound made by the steam, the shrill whistle of the machinery broke in distinctly on the monotonous roar of the cataract; and as this whistling continued, it was evident that it was a signal from the boat to announce its arrival near the falls. The hunter replied by letting off his gun, the report being repeated with a crash by the echoes of the shore. At last the vessel was in sight, and William Emery and his companion were seen by those on board. At a sign from the astronomer the vessel turned, and glided quietly alongside the bank; a rope was thrown ashore, which the bushman seized and twisted round the broken stump of a tree, and immediately a tall man sprang lightly on to the bank, and went towards the astronomer, whilst his companions landed in their turn. William Emery also advanced to meet the stranger, saying inquiringly, "Colonel Everest?"

"Mr. William Emery?" answered the Colonel.

The astronomer bowed and shook hands.

"Gentlemen," then said Colonel Everest, "let me introduce you to Mr. William Emery, of the Cape Town Observatory, who has kindly come as far as the Morgheda Falls to meet us."

Four of the passengers who stood near Colonel Everest bowed to the young astronomer, who did the same; and then the Colonel, with his British self-possession, introduced them officially, saying,—

"Mr. Emery, Sir John Murray, of the county of Devon, your fellow-countryman; Mr. Matthew Strux, of the Poulkowa Observatory; Mr. Nicholas Palander, of the Helsingfors Observatory; and Mr. Michael Zorn, of the Kiew Observatory, three scientific gentlemen who represent the Russian government in our international commission."

Meeting of Members of the Expedition.—[Page 20.]

CHAPTER III.

THE LAND JOURNEY.

THESE introductions over, William Emery put himself at the disposal of the new arrivals, for in his position o astronomer at the Cape, he was inferior in rank to Colonel Everest, a delegate of the English Government, and, with Matthew Strux, joint president of the commission. He knew, as well, that he was a distinguished man of science, famous for his reductions of the nebulæ and his calculations of the occultations of the stars. He was a cold, methodical man, of about fifty years of age, every hour of his life being portioned out with mathematical accuracy. Nothing unforeseen ever happened to him, and his punctuality in every thing was like that of the stars in passing the meridian, and it might be said that all his doings were regulated by the chronometer. William Emery knew all this, and had therefore never doubted that the commission would arrive on the appointed day. During this time he was waiting for the Colonel to tell him the object of this mission to South

Africa; but as he was still silent on the point, Emery thought it better not to ask any questions, as very likely the hour fixed in the Colonel's mind for the subject had not yet come.

Emery also knew by repute the wealthy Sir John Murray, who (almost a rival to Sir James Ross and Lord Elgin) was, although without office, an honour to England by his scientific labours. His pecuniary sacrifices to science were likewise considerable, for he had devoted £20,000 to the establishment of a giant reflector, a match for the telescope at Parson Town, by whose means the elements of a number of double stars had just been determined. He was a man of about forty years of age, with an aristocratic bearing, but whose character it was impossible to discover through his imperturbable exterior.

As to the three Russians, Strux, Palander, and Zorn, their names were also well known to William Emery, although he was not personally acquainted with them. Nicholas Palander and Michael Zorn paid a certain amount of deference to Matthew Strux, as was due to his position, if it had not been to his merit.

The only remark that Emery made was that they were in equal numbers, three English and three Russians; and the crew of the "Queen and Czar" (for that was the name of the steamboat) consisted of ten men, five English and five Russians.

"Mr. Emery," said Colonel Everest, when the introductions were over, "we are now as well acquainted as if we had travelled together from London to Cape Voltas. Besides, your labours have already earned you a just renown, and on that account I hold you in high esteem. It was at my request that the English Government appointed you to assist in our operations in South Africa."

William Emery bowed in acknowledgment, and thought that he was now going to hear the object of the scientific commission to the southern hemisphere; but still Colonel Everest did not explain it.

"Mr. Emery," he went on, "are your preparations complete?"

"Quite, Colonel," replied the astronomer. "According to the directions in Mr. Airy's letter, I left Cape Town a month ago, and went to the station at Lattakoo, and there I collected all the materials for an expedition into the interior of Africa, provisions, waggons, horses, and bushmen. There is an escort of 100 armed men waiting for you at Lattakoo, and they will be under the command of a clever and celebrated hunter, whom I now beg to present to you, the bushman Mokoum."

"The bushman Mokoum!" cried the Colonel (if his usual cold tone could justify such a verb), "the bushman Mokoum! I know his name perfectly well."

"It is the name of a clever, brave African," added Sir

John Murray, turning to the hunter, who was not at all discomposed by the grand airs of the Europeans.

"The hunter Mokoum," said William Emery, as he introduced his companion.

"Your name is well known in the United Kingdom, bushman," replied Colonel Everest. "You were the friend of Anderson and the guide of David Livingstone, whose friend I have the honour of being. I thank you in the name of England, and I congratulate Mr. Emery on having chosen you as the chief of our caravan. Such a hunter as you must be a connoisseur of fire-arms, and as we have a very fair supply, I shall beg you to take your choice of the one which will suit you the best; we know that it will be in good hands."

A smile of satisfaction played round the bushman's lips, for although he was no doubt gratified by the recognition of his services in England, yet the Colonel's offer touched him the most: he then returned thanks in polite terms, and stepped aside, while Emery and the Europeans continued their conversation.

The young astronomer went through all the details of the expedition he had prepared, and the Colonel seemed delighted. He was anxious to reach Lattakoo as quickly as possible, as the caravan ought to start at the beginning of March, after the rainy season.

"Will you be kind enough to decide how you will get to the town, Colonel Everest?" said William Emery.

"The Hunter Mokoum," said William Emery, presenting his Companion.
[Page 24.]

"By the Orange River, and one of its affluents, the Kuruman, which flows close to Lattakoo."

"True," replied the astronomer, "but however well your vessel may travel, it cannot possibly ascend the cataract of Morgheda!"

"We will go round the cataract, Mr. Emery," replied the Colonel, "and by making a land journey of a few miles, we can re-embark above the falls; and from there to Lattakoo, if I am not mistaken, the rivers are navigable for a vessel that does not draw much water."

"No doubt, Colonel," answered William Emery, "but this steamboat is too heavy . . ."

"Mr. Emery," interrupted the Colonel, "this vessel is a masterpiece from Leard and Co's manufactory in Liverpool. It takes to pieces, and is put together again with the greatest ease, a key and a few bolts being all that is required by men used to the work. You brought a waggon to the falls, did you not?"

"Yes, Colonel," answered Emery, "our encampment is not a mile away."

"Well, I must beg the bushman to have the waggon brought to the landing-place, and it will then be loaded with the portions of the vessel and its machinery, which also takes to pieces; and we shall then get up to the spot where the Orange becomes navigable."

Colonel Everest's orders were obeyed. The bushman

disappeared quickly in the underwood, promising to be back in less than an hour, and while he was gone, the steamboat was rapidly unloaded. The cargo was not very considerable; it consisted of some cases of philosophical instruments; a fair collection of guns of Purdey Moore's manufacture, of Edinburgh; some kegs of brandy; some canisters of preserved meat; cases of ammunition; portmanteaus reduced to the smallest size; tent-cloths and all their utensils, looking as if they had come out of a travelling-bazaar; a carefully packed gutta-percha canoe, which took up no more room than a well-folded counterpane; some materials for encamping, &c., &c.; and lastly, a fan-shaped mitrailleuse, a machine not then brought to perfection, but formidable enough to terrify any enemy who might come across their path. All these were placed on the bank; and the engine, of 8-horse power, was divided into three parts: the boiler and its tubes; the mechanism, which was parted from the boiler by a turn of a key; and the screw attached to the false stern-post. When these had been successively carried away, the inside of the vessel was left free. Besides the space reserved for the machinery and the stores, it was divided into a fore-cabin for the use of the crew, and an aft-cabin, occupied by Colonel Everest and his companions. In the twinkling of an eye the partitions vanished, all the chests and bedsteads were lifted out, and now the vessel was reduced to a mere

All these Objects were deposited on the Beach.—[Page 26.]

shell, thirty-five feet long, and composed of three parts, like the "Mâ-Robert," the steam-vessel used by Dr. Livingstone in his first voyage up the Zambesi. It was made of galvanized steel, so that it was light, and at the same time resisting. The bolts, which fastened the plates over a framework of the same metal, kept them firm, and also prevented the possibility of a leakage. William Emery was truly astounded at the simplicity of the work and the rapidity with which it was executed. The waggon, under the guidance of Mokoum and the two Bochjesmen, had only arrived an hour when they were ready to load it. This waggon, rather a primitive vehicle, was mounted on four massive wheels, each couple being about twenty feet apart; it was a regular American "car" in length. This clumsy machine, with its creaking axles projecting a good foot beyond the wheels, was drawn by six tame buffaloes, two and two, who were extremely sensitive to the long goad carried by their driver. It required nothing less than such beasts as these to move the vehicle when heavily laden, for in spite of the adroitness of the "leader," it stuck in the mire more than once. The crew of the "Queen and Czar" now proceeded to load the waggon so as to balance it well every where. The dexterity of sailors is proverbial, and the lading of the vehicle was like play to the brave men. They laid the larger pieces of the boat on the strongest part of the waggon, immediately over the axles of the wheels, so that the cases, chests, barrels, and the lighter and more fragile packages easily found room between them. As to the travellers themselves, a four miles' walk was nothing to them. By three o'clock the loading was finished, and Colonel Everest gave the signal for starting. He and his companions, with William Emery as guide, took the lead, while the bushman, the crew, and the drivers of the waggon followed more slowly. They performed the journey without fatigue, for the slopes that led to the upper course of the Orange made their road easy, by making it longer, and this was a happy thing for the heavily-laden waggon, as it would thus reach its goal more surely, if more slowly.

The different members of the commission clambered lightly up the side of the hill, and the conversation became general, but there was still no mention of the object of the expedition. The Europeans were admiring the splendid scenes that were opened to their view, for this grand nature, so beautiful in its wildness, charmed them as it had charmed the young astronomer, and their voyage had not yet surfeited them with the natural beauties of this African region, though they admired every thing with a quiet admiration, and, English-like, would not do any thing that might seem "improper." However, the cataract drew forth some graceful applause, and although they clapped perhaps with only the tips of their fingers, yet it was enough to show that "nil admirari" was not quite their motto. Besides, William Emery thought it his duty to do the honours of South Africa to his guests; for he was at home, and like certain over-enthusiastic citizens, he did not spare a detail of his African park. Towards half-past four they had passed the cataract of Morgheda, and being now on level ground, the upper part of the river lay before them as far as their eye could reach, and they encamped on the bank to await the arrival of the waggon. It appeared at the top of the hill about five o'clock, having accomplished the journey in safety, and Colonel Everest ordered it to be unloaded immediately, announcing that they were to start at daybreak the next morning. All the night was passed in different occupations. The shell of the vessel was put together again in less than an hour; then the machinery of the screw was put into its place; the metal partitions were fixed between the cabins; the store-rooms were re-furnished, and the different packages neatly arranged on board, and every thing done so quickly that it told a great deal in favour of the crew of the "Queen and Czar." These Englishmen and Russians were picked men, clever and well disciplined, and thoroughly to be depended on. The next day, the 1st of February, the boat was ready to receive its passengers at daybreak. Already there was a volume of black smoke pouring from the funnel, and the engineer, to put the machinery in motion, was causing jets of white steam to fly across the smoke. The machine being at high pressure, without a condenser, the steam escaped at every stroke of the piston, according to the system applied to locomotives; and as to the boiler, with its ingeniously contrived tubes, presenting a large surface to the furnace, it only required half an hour to furnish a sufficient quantity of steam. They had laid in a good stock of ebony and guiacum, which were plentiful in the neighbourhood, and they were now lighting the great fire with this valuable wood.

At six o'clock Colonel Everest gave the signal for starting, and passengers and crew went on board the "Queen and Czar." The hunter, who was acquainted with the course of the river, followed, leaving the two Bochjesmen to take the waggon back to Lattakoo. Just as the vessel was slipping its cable, Colonel Everest turned to the astronomer, and said,—

"By-the-bye, Mr. Emery, you know why we have come here?"

"I have not the least idea, Colonel."

"It is very simple, Mr. Emery: we have come to measure an arc of meridian in South Africa."

CHAPTER IV.

A FEW WORDS ABOUT THE "MÈTRE."

THE idea of an invariable and constant system of measurement, of which nature herself should furnish the exact value, may be said to have existed in the mind of man from the earliest ages. It was of the highest importance, however, that this measurement should be accurately determined, whatever had been the cataclysms of which our earth had been the scene, and it is certain that the ancients felt the same, though they failed in methods and appliances for carrying out the work with sufficient accuracy. The best way of obtaining a constant measurement was to connect it with the terrestrial sphere, whose circumference must be considered as invariable, and then to measure the whole or part of that circumference mathematically. The ancients had tried to do this, and Aristotle, according to some contemporary philosophers, reckoned that the stadium, or Egyptian cubit, formed the hundred-thousandth part of the distance between the pole and the equator, and Eratosthenes, in the time of the Ptolemies, calculated the value of a degree along the Nile, between Syene and Alexandria, pretty correctly; but Posidonius and Ptolemy were not sufficiently accurate in the same kind of geodetic operations that they undertook; neither were their successors.

Picard, for the first time in France, began to regulate the methods that were used for measuring a degree, and in 1669, by measuring the celestial and terrestrial arcs between Paris and Amiens, found that a degree was equal to 57,060 toises, equivalent to 364,876 English feet, or about 69·1 miles. Picard's measurement was continued either way across the French territory as far as Dunkirk and Collioure by Dominic Cassini and Lahire (1683—1718), and it was verified in 1739, from Dunkirk to Perpignan, by Francis Cassini and Lacaille; and at length Méchain carried it as far as Barcelona in Spain; but after his death (for he succumbed to the fatigue attending his operations) the measurement of the meridian in France was interrupted until it was subsequently taken up by Arago and Biot in 1807. These two men prolonged it as far as the Balearic Isles, so that the arc now extended from Dunkirk to Formentera, being equally divided by the parallel of lat. 45° N., half way between the pole and the equator; and under these conditions it was not necessary to take the depression of the earth into account in order to find the value of the quadrant of the meridian. This measurement gave 57,025 toises as the mean value of an arc of a degree in France.

It can be seen that up to that time Frenchmen especially had undertaken to determine that delicate point, and it was likewise the French Convention that, according to Talleyrand's proposition, passed a resolution in 1790, charging the Academy of Sciences to invent an invariable system of weights and measures. Just at that time the statement signed by the illustrious names of Borda, Lagrange, Laplace, Monge, and Condorcet, proposed that the unit of measure should be the *mètre*, the ten-millionth part of the quadrant of the meridian; and that the unit of weight should be the *gramme*, a cubic centimètre of distilled water at the freezing-point; and that the multiples and subdivisions of every measure should be formed decimally.

Later, the determinations of the value of a terrestrial degree were carried on in different parts of the world, for the earth being not spherical, but elliptic, it required much calculation to find the depression at the poles.

In 1736, Maupertuis, Clairaut, Camus, Lemonnier, Outhier, and the Swedish Celsius measured a northern arc in Lapland, and found the length of an arc of a degree to be 57,419 toises. In 1745, La Condamine, Bouguer, and Godin, set sail for Peru, where they were joined by the Spanish officers Juan and Antonio Ulloa, and they then found that the Peruvian arc contained 56,737 toises.

In 1752, Lacaille reported 57,037 toises as the length of the arc he had measured at the Cape of Good Hope.

In 1754, Father Boscowitch and Father le Maire began a survey of the Papal States, and in the course of their operations found the arc between Rome and Rimini to be 56,973 toises.

In 1762 and 1763, Beccaria reckoned the degree in Piedmont at 57,468 toises, and in 1768, the astronomers Mason and Dixon, in North America, on the confines of Maryland and Pennsylvania, found that the value of the degree in America was 56,888 toises.

Since the beginning of the 19th century numbers of other arcs have been measured, in Bengal, the East Indies, Piedmont, Finland, Courland, East Prussia, Denmark, &c., but the English and Russians were less active than other nations in trying to decide this delicate point, their principal geodetic operation being that undertaken by General Roy in 1784, for the purpose of determining the difference of longitude between Paris and Greenwich.

It may be concluded from all the above-mentioned measurements that the mean value of a degree is 57,000 toises, or 25 ancient French leagues, and by multiplying this mean value by the 360 degrees contained in the circumference, it is found that the earth measures 9000 leagues round. But, as may be seen from the figures above, the measurements of the different arcs in different parts of the world do not quite agree. Nevertheless, by taking this average of 57,000 toises for the value of a degree, the value of the mètre, that is to say, the ten-millionth part of the quadrant of the meridian, may be deduced, and is found to be 0.513074 of the whole line, or 39.37079 English inches. In reality, this value is rather too small, for later calculations (taking into account the depression of the earth at the poles, which is $\frac{1}{299.15}$ and not $\frac{1}{314}$, as was thought at first) now give nearly 10,000,856 mètres instead of 10,000,000 for the length of the quadrant of the meridian. The difference of 856 mètres is hardly noticeable in such a long distance; but nevertheless, mathematically speaking, it cannot be said that the mètre, as it is now used, represents the ten-millionth part of the quadrant of the terrestrial meridian exactly; there is an error of about $\frac{1}{5000}$ of a line, i. e. $\frac{1}{5000}$ of the twelfth part of an inch.

The mètre, thus determined, was still not adopted by all the civilized nations. Belgium, Spain, Piedmont, Greece, Holland, the old Spanish colonies, the republics of the Equator, New Granada, and Costa Rica, took a fancy to it immediately; but notwithstanding the evident superiority of this metrical system to every other, England had refused to use it. Perhaps if it had not been for the political disturbances which arose at the close of the 18th century, the inhabitants of the United Kingdom would have accepted the system, for when the Constituent Assembly issued its decree on the 8th of May, 1790, the members of the Royal Society in England were invited to co-operate with the French Academicians. They had to decide whether the measure of the mètre should be founded on the length of the pendulum that beats the sexagesimal second, or whether they should take a fraction of one of the great circles of the earth for a unit of length; but events prevented the proposed conference, and so it was not until the year 1854 that England, having long seen the advantage of the metrical system, and that scientific and commercial societies were being founded to spread the reform, resolved to adopt it. But still the English Government wished to keep their resolution a secret until the new geodetic operations that they had commenced should enable them to assign a more correct value to the terrestrial degree, and they thought they had better act in concert with the Russian Government, who were also hesitating about adopting the system. A Commission of three Englishmen and three Russians was therefore chosen from among the most eminent members of the scientific societies, and we have seen that they were Colonel Everest, Sir John Murray, and William Emery, for England; and Matthew Strux, Nicholas Palander, and Michael Zorn, for Russia. The international Commission having met in London, decided first of all that the measure of an arc of meridian should be taken in the Southern hemisphere, and that another arc should subsequently be measured in the Northern hemisphere, so that from the two operations they might hope to deduce an exact value which should satisfy all the conditions of the programme. It now remained to choose between the different English possessions in the Southern hemisphere, Cape Colony, Australia, and New Zealand. The two last, lying quite at the antipodes of Europe, would involve the Commission in a long voyage, and, besides, the Maoris and Australians, who were often at war with their invaders, might render the proposed operation difficult; while Cape Colony, on the contrary, offered real advantages. In the first place, it was under the same meridian as parts of European Russia, so that after measuring an arc of meridian in South Africa, they could measure a second one in the empire of the Czar, and still keep their operations a secret; secondly, the voyage from England to South Africa was comparatively short; and thirdly, these English and Russian philosophers would find an excellent opportunity there of analyzing the labours of the French astronomer Lacaille, who had worked in the same place, and of proving whether he was correct in giving 57,037 toises as the measurement of a degree of meridian at the Cape of Good Hope. It was therefore decided that the geodetic operation should be commenced at the Cape, and as the two Governments approved of the decision, large credits were opened, and two sets of all the instruments required in a triangulation were manufactured. The astronomer William Emery was asked to make preparations for an exploration in the interior of South Africa, and the frigate "Augusta," of the royal navy, received orders to convey the members of the Commission and their suite to the mouth of the Orange River.

It should here be added, that besides the scientific question, there was also a question of national vainglory that excited these philosophers to join in a common labour; for, in reality, they were anxious to out-do France in her numerical calculations, and to surpass in precision the labours of her most illustrious astronomers, and that in the heart of a savage and almost unknown land. Thus the members of the Anglo-Russian Commission had resolved to sacrifice every thing, even their lives, in order to obtain a result that should be favourable to science, and at the same time glorious for their country. And this is how it came to pass that the astronomer William Emery found himself at the Morgheda Falls, on the banks of the Orange River, at the end of January, 1854.

CHAPTER V.

A HOTTENTOT VILLAGE.

THE voyage along the upper course of the river was soon accomplished, and although the weather soon became rainy, the passengers, comfortably installed in the ship's cabin, suffered no inconvenience from the torrents of rain which usually fall at that season. The "Queen and Czar" shot along rapidly, for there were neither rapids nor shallows, and the current was not sufficiently strong to retard her progress. Every aspect of the river-banks was enchanting; forest followed upon forest, and quite a world of birds dwelt among the leafy branches. Here and there were groups of trees belonging to the family of the "proteaceæ," and especially the "wagenboom" with its reddish marbled-wood forming a curious contrast with its deep blue leaves and large pale yellow flowers: then there were the "zwartebasts" with their black bark, and the "karrees" with dark evergreen foliage. The banks were shaded every where by weeping willows, while the underwood extended beyond for several miles. Every now and then vast open tracks presented themselves unexpectedly, large plains, covered with innumerable colocynths, mingled with "sugar-bushes," out of which flew clouds of sweet-singing little birds, called "suiker-vogels" by the Cape colonists. The winged world offered many varieties, all of which were pointed out to Sir John Murray by the bushman. Sir John was a great lover of game, both hairy and feathered, and thus a sort of intimacy arose between him and Mokoum, to whom, according to Colonel Everest's promise, he had given an excellent long-range rifle, made on the Pauly system. It would be useless to attempt a description of the bushman's delight when he found himself in possession of such a splendid weapon. The two hunters understood each other well, for though so learned, Sir John Murray passed for one of the most brilliant fox-hunters in old Caledonia, and he listened to the bushman's stories with an interest amounting to envy. His eyes sparkled when Mokoum showed him the wild ruminants in the woods; here a herd of fifteen to twenty giraffes; there, buffaloes six feet high, with towering black horns: farther on, fierce gnus with horses' tails; and again, herds of "caamas," a large kind of deer, with bright eyes, and horns forming a threatening-looking triangle; and every where, in the dense forests as well as in the open plains, the innumerable varieties of antelopes which abound in Southern Africa; the spurious chamois, the gems-bok, the gazelle, the duiker-bok, and the spring-bok. Was not all this something to tempt a hunter, and could the fox-hunts of the Scottish lowlands vie with the exploits of a Cumming, an Anderson, or a Baldwin? It must be confessed that Sir John Murray's companions were less excited than himself at these magnificent specimens of wild game. William Emery was watching his colleagues attentively, and trying to discover their character under their cold exterior. Colonel Everest and Matthew Strux, men of about the same age, were equally cold, reserved, and formal; they always spoke with a measured slowness, and from morning to night it seemed as if they had never met before. That any intimacy should ever be established between two such important personages was a thing not to be hoped for; two icebergs, placed side by side would join in time, but two scientific men, each holding a high position, never.

Nicholas Palander, a man of about fifty-five years of age, was one of those who have never been young, and who will never be old. The astronomer of Helsingfors, constantly absorbed in his calculations, might be a very admirably constructed machine, but still he was nothing but a machine, a kind of abacus, or universal reckoner. He was the calculator of the Anglo-Russian Commission, and one of those prodigies who work out multiplications to five figures in their head, like a fifty-year-old Mondeux.

Michael Zorn more nearly resembled William Emery in age, enthusiasm, and good humour. His amiable qualities did not prevent his being an astronomer of great merit, having attained an early celebrity. The discoveries made by him at the Kiew Observatory concerning the nebula of Andromeda had attracted attention in scientific Europe, and yet with this undoubted merit he had a great deal of modesty, and was always in the background. William Emery and Michael Zorn were becoming great friends, united by the same tastes and aspirations; and most generally they were talking together, while Colonel Everest and Matthew Strux were coldly watching each other, and Palander was mentally extracting cube roots without noticing the lovely scenes on the banks, and Sir John Murray and the bushman were forming plans for hunting down whole hecatombs of victims.

No incident marked the voyage along the upper course of the Orange. Sometimes the granite cliffs which shut in the winding bed of the river seemed to forbid further progress, and often the wooded islands which dotted the current seemed to render the route uncertain; but the bushman never hesitated, and the "Queen and Czar" always chose the right route, and passed round the cliffs without hindrance. The helmsman never had to repent of having followed Mokoum's directions.

In four days the steamboat had passed over the 240 miles

between the cataract of Morgheda and the Kuruman, an affluent which flowed exactly past the town of Lattakoo, whither Colonel Everest's expedition was bound. About thirty leagues above the falls the river bends from its general direction, which is east and west, and flows southeast as far as the acute angle which the territory of Cape Colony makes in the north, and then turning to the northeast, it loses itself in the wooded country of the Transvaal Republic. It was early in the morning of the 5th of February, in a driving rain, that the "Queen and Czar" arrived at Klaarwater, a Hottentot village, close to the meeting of the Orange and Kuruman. Colonel Everest, unwilling to lose a moment, passed quickly by the few Bochjesmen cabins that form the village, and under the pressure of her screw, the vessel began to ascend the affluent. The rapid current was to be attributed, as the passengers remarked, to a peculiarity in the river, for the Kuruman being wide at its source, was lessened as it descended by the influence of the sun's rays; but at this season, swollen by the rains, and further increased by the waters of a sub-affluent, the Moschona, it became very deep and rapid. The fires were therefore made up, and the vessel ascended the Kuruman at the rate of three miles an hour.

During the voyage the bushman pointed out a good many hippopotami in the water; but these great pachyderms, clumsy, thickset beasts, from eight to ten feet long, which the Dutch at the Cape call "sea-cows," were by no means of an aggressive nature, and the hissing of the steam and the panting of the screw quite frightened them, the boat appearing to them like some great monster which they ought to distrust, and in fact, the arsenal on board would have rendered approach very difficult. Sir John Murray would have very much liked to try his explosive bullets on the fleshy masses, but the bushman assured him that there would be no lack of hippopotami in the more northerly rivers, so he determined to wait for a more favourable opportunity.

The 150 miles which separated the mouth of the Kuruman from the station of Lattakoo were traversed in fifty hours, and on the 7th of February the travellers had reached the end of their journey. As soon as the steamboat was moored to the bank which served as a quay, a man of fifty years of age, with a grave air but kind countenance, stepped on board, and offered his hand to William Emery. The astronomer introduced the new-comer to his travelling companions, as—

"The Rev. Thomas Dale, of the London Missionary Society, Governor of the station of Lattakoo."

The Europeans bowed to Mr. Dale, who gave them welcome, and put himself at their service.

The town of Lattakoo, or rather the village of that name,

The Mission Home Establishment.—[Page 44.]

is the most northerly of the Cape Missionary stations, and is divided into Old and New. The first, which the "Queen and Czar" now reached, had 12,000 inhabitants at the beginning of the century, but they have since emigrated to the north-east, and the town, now fallen into decay, has been replaced by New Lattakoo, which is built close by, on a plain which was formerly covered with acacias, and thither Mr. Dale conducted the Europeans. It consisted of about forty groups of houses, and contained 5000 or 6000 inhabitants of the tribe of the Bechuanas. Dr. Livingstone stayed in this town for three months before his first voyage up the Zambesi in 1840, previously to crossing the whole of Central Africa, from the bay of Loanda to the port of Kilmana on the coast of Mozambique.

When they reached New Lattakoo, Colonel Everest presented a letter from Dr. Livingstone, which commended the Anglo-Russian Commission to his friends in South Africa. Mr. Dale read it with much pleasure, and returned it to the Colonel, saying that he might find it useful on his journey, as the name of David Livingstone was known and honoured throughout that part of Africa.

The members of the Commission were lodged in the missionary establishment, a large house built on an eminence and surrounded by an impenetrable hedge like a fortification. The Europeans could be more comfortably lodged here than with the Bechuanas; not that their dwellings were not kept properly in order; on the contrary, the smooth clay floors did not show a particle of dust, and the long-thatched roofs were quite rain-proof; but at best, their houses were little better than huts with a round hole for a door, hardly large enough to admit a man; moreover, they all lived in common, and close contact with the Bechuanas would scarcely have been agreeable.

The chief of the tribe, one Moulibahan, lived at Lattakoo, and thought it right to come and pay his respects to the Europeans. He was rather a fine man, without the thick lips and flat nose of the negro, with a round face not so shrunken in its lower part as that of the other Hottentots. He was dressed in a cloak of skins, sewn together with considerable art, and an apron called a "pujoke." He wore a leather skull-cap, and sandals of ox-hide: ivory rings were wound round his arms, and from his ears hung brass plates about four inches long—a kind of ear-ring—which is also a charm; an antelope's tail stood up in his skull-cap, and his hunting-stick was surmounted by a tuft of small black ostrich feathers. The natural colour of his body was quite invisible through the thick coating of ochre with which he was besmeared from head to foot, while some ineffaceable incisions in his legs denoted the number of enemies he had slain.

The chief, as grave as Matthew Strux himself, stepped

Chief Moulibahan.—[Page 46.]

up to the Europeans, and took them in turn by the nose. The Russians permitted this to be done quite gravely, the English rather more reluctantly, but still it had to be done, for according to African custom, it denoted a solemn engagement to fulfil the duties of hospitality to the Europeans. When the ceremony was over, Moulibahan retired without having uttered a word.

"And now that we are naturalized Bechuanas," said Colonel Everest, "let us begin our operations without losing a day or an hour."

And indeed no time was lost; still, such is the variety of detail required in the organization of an expedition of this character, the Commission was not ready to start until the beginning of March. That, however, was the time appointed by Colonel Everest; because then the rainy season just being over, the water, preserved in the fissures of the earth, would furnish a valuable resource to travellers in the desert.

On the 2nd of March, then, the whole caravan, under Mokoum's command, was ready. The Europeans took farewell of the missionaries at Lattakoo, and left the village at seven o'clock in the morning.

"Where are we going, Colonel?" asked William Emery, as the caravan passed the last house in the town.

"Straight on, Mr. Emery," answered the Colonel, "until we reach a suitable place for establishing a base."

At eight o'clock the caravan had passed over the low shrubby hills which skirt the town, and soon the desert, with its dangers, fatigues, and risks, lay unfolded before the travellers.

CHAPTER VI.

BETTER ACQUAINTANCE.

THE escort under the bushman's command was composed of 100 men, all Bochjesmen—an industrious, good-tempered people, capable of enduring great physical fatigue. In former times, before the arrival of the missionaries, these Bochjesmen were a lying, inhospitable race, thinking of nothing but murder and pillage, and ever taking advantage of an enemy's sleep to massacre him. To a great extent the missionaries have modified these barbarous habits, but the natives are still more or less farm-pillagers and cattle-lifters.

Ten waggons, like the vehicle which Mokoum had taken to the Morgheda Falls, formed the bulk of the expedition. Two of these were like moving houses, fitted up as they were with a certain amount of comfort, and served as an encampment for the Europeans; so that Colonel Everest and his companions were followed about by a wooden habitation with dry flooring, and well tilted with water-

E

proof cloth, and furnished with beds and toilet furniture. Thus, on arriving at each place of encampment, the tent was always ready pitched. Of these waggons, one was appropriated to Colonel Everest and his countrymen, Sir John Murray and William Emery: the other was used by the Russians, Matthew Strux, Nicholas Palander, and Michael Zorn. Two more, arranged in the same way, belonged, one to the five Englishmen and the other to the five Russians who composed the crew of the "Queen and Czar."

The hull and machinery of the steamboat, taken to pieces and laid on one of the waggons, followed the travellers, in case the Commission might come across some of the numerous lakes which are found in the interior of the continent.

The remaining waggons carried the tools, provisions, baggage, arms, and ammunition, as well as the instruments required for the proposed triangular survey. The provisions of the Bochjesmen consisted principally of antelope, buffalo, or elephant meat, preserved in long strips, being dried in the sun or by a slow fire: thus economizing the use of salt, here very scarce. In the place of bread, the Bochjesmen depended on the earth-nuts of the arachis, the bulbs of various species of mesembryanthemums, and other native productions. Animal food would be provided by the hunters of the party, who, adroitly employing their bows and lances, would scour the plains and revictual the caravan.

Six native oxen, long-legged, high-shouldered, and with great horns, were attached to each waggon with harness of buffalo hide. Thus the primitive vehicles moved slowly though surely on their massive wheels, ready alike for heights or valleys. For the travellers to ride there were provided small black or grey Spanish horses, good-tempered, brave animals, imported from South America, and much esteemed at the Cape. Among the troops of quadrupeds were also half-a-dozen tame quaggas, a kind of ass with plump bodies and slender legs, who make a noise like the barking of a dog. They were to be used in the smaller expeditions necessary to the geodetic operations, and were adapted to carry the instruments where the waggons could not venture. The only exception to the others was the bushman, who rode a splendid zebra with remarkable grace and dexterity. This animal (the beauty of whose coat with its brown stripes especially excited the admiration of the connoisseur Sir John Murray) was naturally defiant and suspicious, and would not have borne any other rider than Mokoum, who had broken it in for his own use. Some dogs of a half-savage breed, sometimes wrongly called "hyena-hunters," ran by the side of the waggons, their shape and long ears reminding one of the European brach-hound.

Such was the caravan which was about to bury itself in the deserts. The oxen advanced calmly under the guidance of their drivers, ever and again pricking them in the flank with their "jambox;" and it was strange to see the troop winding along the hills in marching order. After leaving Lattakoo, whither was the expedition going? Colonel Everest had said, "Straight on;" and indeed he and Matthew Strux could not yet follow a fixed course. What they wanted, before commencing their trigonometrical operations, was a vast level plain, on which to establish the base of the first of the triangles, which, like a network, were to cover for several degrees the southern part of Africa. The Colonel explained to the bushman what he wanted, and with the calmness of one to whom scientific language is familiar, talked to him of triangles, adjacent angles, bases, meridians, zenith distances, and the like. Mokoum let him go on for a few moments, then interrupted him with an impatient movement, saying, "Colonel, I don't know any thing about your angles, bases, and meridians. I don't understand even in the least what you are going to do in the desert: but that is your business. You are asking for a large level plain; oh well, I can find you that."

And at his orders, the caravan, having just ascended the Lattakoo hills, turned down again towards the south-west. This took them rather more to the south of the village,

William Emery and Michael Zorn in advance of the Expedition.—[Page 53.]

towards the plain watered by the Kuruman, and here the bushman expected to find a suitable place for the Colonel's plans. From that day, he always took the head of the caravan. Sir John Murray, well mounted, never left him, and from time to time the report of a gun made his colleagues aware that he was making acquaintance with the African game. The Colonel, quite absorbed in contemplating the difficulties of the expedition, let his horse carry him on. Matthew Strux, sometimes on horseback, sometimes in the waggon, according to the nature of the ground, seldom opened his lips. Nicholas Palander, as bad a rider as could be, was generally on foot; at other times he shut himself up in his vehicle, and there lost himself in the profoundest mathematical abstractions.

Although William Emery and Michael Zorn occupied separate waggons at night, they were always together when the caravan was on the march. Every day and every incident of the journey bound them in a closer friendship. From one stage to another they rode, talked, and argued together. Sometimes they fell behind the train, and sometimes rode on several miles ahead of it, when the plain extended as far as they could see. They were free here and lost amidst the wildness of nature. How they forgot figures and problems, calculations and observations, and chatted of every thing but science! They were no longer astronomers contemplating the starry firmament, but were more like two youths escaped from school, revelling in the dense forests and boundless plains. They laughed like ordinary mortals. Both of them had excellent dispositions, open, amiable, and devoted, forming a strange contrast to Colonel Everest and Matthew Strux, who were formal, not to say stiff. These two chiefs were often the subject of their conversation, and Emery learnt a good deal about them from his friend.

"Yes," said Michael Zorn, that day, "I watched them well on board the 'Augusta,' and I profess I think they are jealous of each other. And if Colonel Everest appears to be at the head of things, Matthew Strux is not less than his equal: the Russian Government has clearly established his position. One chief is as imperious as the other; and besides, I tell you again, there is the worst of all jealousy between them, the jealousy of the learned."

"And that for which there is the least occasion," answered Emery, "because in discoveries every thing has its value, and each one derives equal benefit. But, my dear Zorn, if, as I believe, your observations are correct, it is unfortunate for our expedition: in such a work there ought to be a perfect understanding."

"No doubt," replied Zorn, "and I fear that that understanding does not exist. Think of our confusion, if every detail, the choice of a base, the method of calculating, the position of the stations, the verification of the figures, opens a fresh discussion every time! Unless I am much mistaken I forbode a vast deal of quibbling when we come to compare our registers, and the observations we shall have made to the minutest fraction."

"You frighten me," said Emery. "It would be sorrowful to carry an enterprise of this kind so far, and then to fail for want of concord. Let us hope that your fears may not be realized."

"I hope they may not," answered the young Russian; "but I say again, I assisted at certain scientific discussions on the voyage, which showed me that both Colonel Everest and his rival are undeniably obstinate, and that at heart there is a miserable jealousy between them."

"But these two gentlemen are never apart," observed Emery. "You never find one without the other; they are as inseparable as ourselves."

"True," replied Zorn, "they are never apart all day long, but then they never exchange ten words: they only keep watch on each other. If one doesn't manage to annihilate the other, we shall indeed work under deplorable conditions."

"And for yourself," asked William, hesitatingly, "which of the two would you wish——"

"My dear William," replied Zorn with much frankness, "I shall loyally accept him as chief who can command respect as such. This is a question of science, and I have no prejudice in the matter. Matthew Strux and the Colonel are both remarkable and worthy men: England and Russia should profit equally from their labours; therefore it matters little whether the work is directed by an Englishman or a Russian. Are you not of my opinion?"

"Quite," answered Emery; "therefore do not let us be distracted by absurd prejudices, and let us as far as possible use our efforts for the common good. Perhaps it will be possible to ward off the blows of the two adversaries; and besides there is your fellow countryman, Nicholas Palander——"

"He!" laughed Zorn, "he will neither see, hear, nor comprehend any thing! He would make calculations to any extent; but he is neither Russian, Prussian, English, or Chinese; he is not even an inhabitant of this sublunary sphere; he is Nicholas Palander, that's all."

"I cannot say the same for my countryman, Sir John Murray," said Emery. "He is a thorough Englishman, and a most determined hunter, and he would sooner follow the traces of an elephant and giraffe than give himself any trouble about a scientific argument. We must therefore depend upon ourselves, Zorn, to neutralize the antipathy between our chiefs. Whatever happens, we must hold together."

"Ay, whatever happens," replied Zorn, holding out his hand to his friend.

The bushman still continued to guide the caravan down

towards the south-west. At midday, on the 4th of March, it reached the base of the long wooded hills which extend from Lattakoo. Mokoum was not mistaken; he had led the expedition towards the plain, but it was still undulated, and therefore unfitted for an attempt at triangulation. The march continued uninterrupted, and Mokoum rode at the head of the riders and waggons, while Sir John Murray, Emery, and Zorn pushed on in advance. Towards the end of the day, they all arrived at a station occupied by one of the wandering "boers," or farmers, who are induced by the richness of the pasture-land to make temporary abodes in various parts of the country.

The colonist, a Dutchman, and head of a large family, received the Colonel and his companions most hospitably, and would take no remuneration in return. He was one of those brave, industrious men, whose slender capital, intelligently employed in the breeding of oxen, cows, and goats, soon produces a fortune. When the pasturage is exhausted, the farmer, like a patriarch of old, seeks for new springs and fertile prairies, pitching his camp afresh where the conditions seem favourable.

The farmer opportunely told Colonel Everest of a wide plain, fifteen miles away, which would be found quite flat. The caravan started next morning at daybreak. The only incident that broke the monotony of the long morning march, was Sir John Murray's taking a shot, at a distance of more than 1000 yards, at a gnu, a curious animal about five feet high, with the muzzle of an ox, a long white tail, and pointed horns. It fell with a heavy groan, much to the astonishment of the bushman, who was surprised at seeing the animal struck at such a distance. The gnu generally affords a considerable quantity of excellent meat, and was accordingly in high esteem among the hunters of the caravan.

The site indicated by the farmer was reached about midday. It was a boundless prairie stretching to the north without the slightest undulation. No better spot for measuring a base could be imagined, and the bushman, after a short investigation, returned to Colonel Everest with the announcement that they had reached the place they were seeking.

The Bushman pointing to the Plain.—[Page 58.]

CHAPTER VII.

THE BASE OF THE TRIANGLE.

THE work undertaken by the Commission was a triangulation for the purpose of measuring an arc of meridian. Now the direct measurement of one or more degrees by means of metal rods would be impracticable. In no part of the world is there a region so vast and unbroken as to admit of so delicate an operation. Happily, there is an easier way of proceeding by dividing the region through which the meridian passes into a number of imaginary triangles, whose solution is comparatively easy.

These triangles are obtained by observing signals, either natural or artificial, such as church-towers, posts, or reverberatory lamps, by means of the theodolite or repeating-circle. Every signal is the vertex of a triangle, whose angles are exactly determined by the instruments, so that a good observer with a proper telescope can take the bearings of any object whatever, a tower by day, or a lamp by night. Sometimes the sides of the triangles are many miles in length, and when Arago connected the coast of

Valencia in Spain with the Balearic Islands, one of the sides measured 422,555 toises. When one side and two angles of any triangle are known, the other sides and angle may be found; by taking, therefore, a side of one of the known triangles for a new base, and by measuring the angles adjacent to the base, new triangles can be successively formed along the whole length of the arc; and since every straight line in the network of triangles is known, the length of the arc can be easily determined. The values of the sides and angles may be obtained by the theodolite and repeating circle, but the *first* side, the base of the whole system, must be actually measured on the ground, and this operation requires the utmost care.

When Delambre and Méchain measured the meridian of France from Dunkirk to Barcelona, they took for their base a straight line, 12,150 mètres in length, in the road from Melun to Licusaint, and they were no less than 42 days in measuring it. Colonel Everest and Matthew Strux designed proceeding in the same way, and it will be seen how much precision was necessary.

The work was begun on the 5th of March, much to the astonishment of the Bochjesmen, who could not at all understand it. Mokoum thought it strange for these learned men to measure the earth with rods six feet long; but any way, he had done his duty; they had asked him for a level plain, and he had found it for them.

Commencement of the Geodesic Operations.—[Page 61.]

The place was certainly well chosen. Covered with dry, short grass, the plain was perfectly level as far as the horizon. Behind lay a line of hills forming the southern boundary of the Kalahari desert; towards the north the plain seemed boundless. To the east, the sides of the table-land of Lattakoo disappeared in gentle slopes; and in the west, where the ground was lower, the soil became marshy, as it imbibed the stagnant water which fed the affluents of the Kuruman.

"I think, Colonel Everest," said Strux, after he had surveyed the grassy level, "that when our base is established, we shall be able here also to fix the extremity of our meridian."

"Likely enough," replied the Colonel. "We must find out too, whether the arc meets with any obstacles that may impede the survey. Let us measure the base, and we will decide afterwards whether it will be better to join it by a series of auxiliary triangles to those which the arc must cross."

They thus resolved to proceed to the measurement of the base. It would be a long operation, for they wanted to obtain even more correct results than those obtained by the French philosophers at Melun. This would be a matter of some difficulty: since when a new base was measured afterwards near Perpignan to verify the calculations, there was only an error of 11 inches in a distance of 330,000 toises.

Orders were given for encamping, and a Bochjesman village, a kind of kraal, was formed on the plain. The waggons were arranged in a circle like the houses, the English and Russian flags floating over their respective quarters. The centre was common ground. The horses and buffaloes, which by day grazed outside, were driven in by night to the interior, to save them from attacks of the wild beasts around.

Mokoum took upon himself to arrange the hunting expedition for revictualling; and Sir John Murray, whose presence was not indispensable in the measurement of the base, looked after the provisions, and served out the rations of preserved meat and fresh venison. Thanks to the skill and experience of Mokoum and his companions, game was never wanting. They scoured the district for miles round, and the report of their guns resounded at all hours.

The survey began on the next day, Zorn and Emery being charged with the preliminaries.

"Come along," said Zorn, "and good luck be with us."

The primary operation consisted in tracing a line on the ground where it was especially level. This chanced to be from S.E. to N.W., and pickets being placed at short intervals to mark the direction, Zorn carefully verified the correctness of their position by means of the thread-wires of his telescope. For more than eight miles (the proposed length of the base) was the measurement continued, and the young men performed their work with scrupulous fidelity.

The next step was to adjust the rods for the actual measurement, apparently a very simple operation, but which, in fact, demands the most continuous caution, as the success of a triangulation in a great measure is contingent on its preciseness.

On the morning of the 10th, twelve wooden pedestals were planted along the line, securely fastened in their position, and prepared to support the rods. Colonel Everest and Matthew Strux, assisted by their young coadjutors, placed the rods in position, and Nicholas Palander stood ready, pencil in hand, to write down in a double register the figures transmitted to him.

The rods employed were six in number, and exactly two toises in length. They were made of platinum, as being (under ordinary circumstances) unaffected by any condition of the atmosphere. In order, however, to provide against any change of temperature, each was covered with a rod of copper somewhat shorter than itself, and a microscopic vernier was attached, to indicate any contraction or expansion that might occur. The rods were next placed lengthwise, with a small interval between each, in order to avoid the slight shock which might result from immediate contact. Colonel Everest and Matthew Strux with their own hands placed the first rod. About a hundred toises farther on, they had marked a point of sight, and as the rods were each provided with iron projections, it was not difficult to place them exactly in the proper direction. Emery and Zorn, lying on the ground, saw that the projections stood exactly in the middle of the sight.

"Now," said Colonel Everest, "we must define our exact starting-point. We will drop a line from the end of our first rod, and that will definitely mark the extremity of our base."

"Yes," answered Strux, "but we must take into account the radius of the line."

"Of course," said the Colonel.

The starting-point determined, the work went on. The next proceeding was to determine the inclination of the base with the horizon.

"We do not, I believe, pretend," said Colonel Everest, "to place the rod in a position which is perfectly horizontal."

"No," answered Strux, "it is enough to find the angle which each rod makes with the horizon, and we can then deduce the true inclination."

Thus agreed, they proceeded with their observations, employing their spirit-level, and testing every result by the vernier. As Palander was about to inscribe the record, Strux requested that the level should be reversed, in order that by the division of the two registers a closer approximation to truth might be attained. This mode of double observation was continued throughout the operations.

Two important points were now obtained: the direction of the rod with regard to the base, and the angle which it made with the horizon. The results were inscribed in two registers, and signed by the members of the Commission.

There were still two further observations, no less important, to be made: the variation of the rod caused by differences of temperature, and the exact distance measured by it. The former was easily determined by comparing the difference in length between the platinum and copper rods. The microscope gave the variation of the platinum, and this was entered in the double register, to be afterwards reduced to 16° Centigrade.

They had now to observe the distance actually measured. To obtain this result, it was necessary to place the second rod at the end of the first, leaving a small space between them. When the second rod was adjusted with the same care as the former, it only remained to measure the interval between the two. A small tongue of platinum, known as a slider, was attached to the end of the platinum bar that was not covered by the copper, and this Colonel Everest slipped gently along until it touched the next rod. The slider was marked off into 10,000ths of a toise, and as a vernier with its microscope gave the 100,000ths, the space could be very accurately determined. The result was immediately registered.

Michael Zorn, considering that the covered platinum

F

might be sooner affected by heat than the uncovered copper, suggested another precaution: accordingly they erected a small awning to protect the rod from the sun's rays.

For more than a month were these minutiæ patiently carried on. As soon as four bars were adjusted, and the requisite observations complete, the last of the rods was carried to the front. It was impossible to measure more than 220 to 230 toises a day, and sometimes, when the wind was violent, operations were altogether suspended.

Every evening, about three quarters of an hour before it became too dark to read the verniers, they left off work, after taking various anxious precautions. They brought forward temporarily the rod "No. 1," and marked the point of its termination. Here they made a hole, and drove in a stake with a leaden plate attached. They then replaced "No. 1" in its original position, after observing the inclination, the thermometric variation, and the direction. They noted the prolongation measured by rod "No. 4," and then with a plumb-line touching the foremost end of rod "No. 1," they made a mark on the leaden plate. They carefully traced through this point two lines at right angles, one signifying the base, the other the perpendicular. The plate was then covered with a wooden lid, the hole filled in, and the stake left buried till the morning. Thus, if any accident had happened to their apparatus during the night they would not be obliged to begin afresh. The next day, the plate was uncovered, and rod "No. 1" replaced in the same position as on the evening before, by means of the plumb-line, whose point ought to fall exactly on the point intersected by the two straight lines.

These operations were carried on for thirty-eight days along the plain, and every figure was registered doubly, and verified, compared, and approved, by each member of the Commission.

Few discussions arose between Colonel Everest and his Russian colleague; and if sometimes the smallest fraction of a toise gave occasion for some polite cavillings, they always yielded to the opinion of the majority. One question alone called for the intervention of Sir John Murray. This was about the length of the base. It was certain that the longer the base, the easier would be the measurement of the opposite angle. Colonel Everest proposed 6000 toises, nearly the same as the base measured at Melun; but Matthew Strux wished that it should be 10,000 toises, since the ground permitted. Colonel Everest, however, remained firm, and Strux seemed equally determined not to yield. After a few plausible arguments, personalities began: they were no longer two astronomers, but an Englishman and a Russian. Happily the debate was interrupted by some days of bad weather, which allowed their tempers to cool. It was subsequently decided by the majority that they should "split the difference," and assign 8000 toises as the measurement of the base. The work was at length completed. Any error which occurred, in spite of their extreme precision, might be afterwards corrected by measuring a new base from the northern extremity of the meridian.

The base measured exactly 8037.75 toises, and upon this they were now to place their series of triangles.

Measuring the Arc of the Meridian.—[Page 69.]

Taking the Measurements. — [Page 69.]

CHAPTER VIII.

THE TWENTY-FOURTH MERIDIAN.

THE measurement of the base occupied thirty-eight days, from the 6th of March to the 13th of April, and without loss of time the chiefs decided to begin the triangles. The first operation was to find the southern extremity of the arc, and the same being done at the northern extremity, the difference would give the number of degrees measured.

On the 14th they began to find their latitude. Emery and Zorn had already on the preceding nights taken the altitude of numerous stars, and their work was so accurate that the greatest error was not more than 2″, and even this was probably owing to the refraction caused by the changes in the atmospheric strata. The latitude thus carefully sought was found to be $27.951789°$. They then found the longitude, and marked the spot on an excellent large scale map of South Africa, which showed the most recent geographical discoveries, and also the routes of travellers and naturalists, such as Livingstone, Anderson, Magyar, Baldwin,

Burchell, and Lichtenstein. They then had to choose on what meridian they would measure their arc. The longer this arc is the less influence have the errors in the determination of latitude. The arc from Dunkirk to Formentera, on the meridian of Paris, was exactly 9° 56'. They had to choose their meridian with great circumspection. Any natural obstacles, such as mountains or large tracts of water, would seriously impede their operations; but happily, this part of Africa seemed well suited to their purpose, since the risings in the ground were inconsiderable, and the few watercourses easily traversed. Only dangers, and not obstacles, need check their labours.

This district is occupied by the Kalahari desert, a vast region extending from the Orange River to Lake Ngami, from lat. 20° S. to lat. 29°. In width, it extends from the Atlantic on the west as far as long. 25° E. Dr. Livingstone followed its extreme eastern boundary when he travelled as far as Lake Ngami and the Zambesi Falls. Properly speaking, it does not deserve the name of desert. It is not like the sands of Sahara, which are devoid of vegetation, and almost impassable on account of their aridity. The Kalahari produces many plants; its soil is covered with abundant grass; it contains dense groves and forests; animals abound, wild game and beasts of prey; and it is inhabited and traversed by sedentary and wandering tribes of Bushmen and Bakalaharis. But the true obstacle to its exploration is the dearth of water which prevails through the greater part of the year, when the rivers are dried up. However, at this time, just at the end of the rainy season, they could depend upon considerable reservoirs o. stagnant water, preserved in pools and rivulets. Such were the particulars given by Mokoum. He had often visited the Kalahari, sometimes on his own account as a hunter, and sometimes as a guide to some geographical exploration.

It had now to be actually considered whether the meridian should be taken from one of the extremities of the base, thus avoiding a series of auxiliary triangles[1].

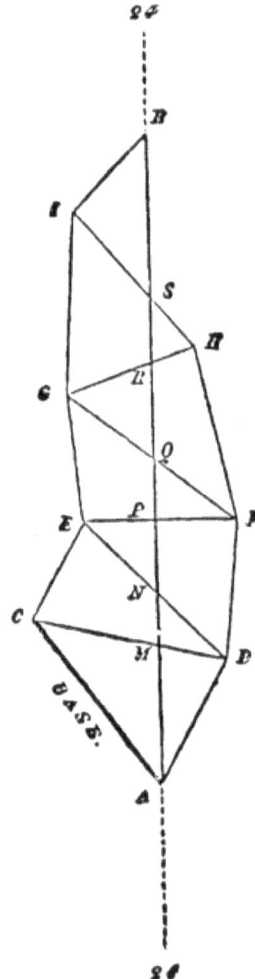

[1] By the aid of the accompanying figure, the work called a triangulation may be understood. Let A B be the arc. Measure the base A C very carefully from the extremity A to the first station C. Take other stations, D, E, F, G, H, I, &c., on alternate sides of the meridian, and observe the angles of the triangles, A C D, C D E, D E F, E F G, &c. Then in the triangle A C D, the angles and the side A C being known, the side C D may be found. Likewise in the triangle C D E, C D and the angles being known, the side D E may be found; and so on through all the triangles. Now determine the direction of the meridian in the ordinary way, and observe the angle M A C which it makes with the base A C.

After some discussion, it was decided that the southern extremity of the base would serve for a starting-point. It was the twenty-fourth meridian east from Greenwich, and extended over seven degrees of latitude, from 20° to 27°, without any apparent natural obstacle. Towards the north it certainly crossed the eastern end of Lake Ngami, but Arago had met with greater difficulties than this when he applied his geodesy to connect the coast of Spain with the Balearic Islands. It was accordingly decided that meridian 24° should be measured, since, if it were afterwards prolonged into Europe, a northern arc of the same meridian might be measured on Russian territory.

The astronomers proceeded at once to choose a station which should form the vertex of the first triangle. This was a solitary tree to the right of the meridian, standing on a mound about ten miles away. It was distinctly visible from each extremity of the base, and its slender top facilitated the taking of its bearings. The angle made by the tree with the south-east extremity of the base was first

Then in the triangle A C M, because A C and the adjacent angles are known, A M, C M, and the angle A C M, may be found, and A M is the first portion of the arc. Then in the triangle D M N, since the side D M = C D — C M, and the adjacent angles are known, the sides M N, D N, and the angle M N D may be found, and M N is the next portion of the arc. Again, in the triangle N E P, because E N = D E — D N, and the adjacent angles are known, N P, the third portion of the arc, may be found. By proceeding thus through all the triangles, piece by piece, the whole length of the arc A B may be determined.

The Astronomers at Work.—[Page 72.]

observed, with the help of one of Borda's repeating circles.

The two telescopes were adjusted so that their axes were exactly in the plane of the circle, in such a way that their position represented the angular distance between the tree and the north-west extremity of the base. This admirably-constructed instrument corrects nearly all the errors of observation, and indeed, if the repetitions are numerous, the errors tend to counterbalance and correct each other.

The Commission had four repeating circles: two for measuring angles, and two more with vertical circles for obtaining zenith distances, and so calculating in a single night, to the smallest fraction of a second, the latitude of any station. And indeed, in this important survey, it was not only necessary to obtain the value of the angles of the triangles, but also to measure the meridian altitude of the stars, that being equal to the latitude of each station.

The work began on the 14th of April. Colonel Everest, Zorn, and Palander observed the angle at the south-east extremity of the base, while Strux, Emery, and Sir John Murray observed that at the north-west extremity.

Meantime the camp was raised, and the bullocks harnessed, and Mokoum conducted the caravan to the first station as a halting-place. Two caravans, with their drivers, accompanied the observers, to carry the instruments. The weather was bright, but had the atmosphere been unfavourable by day, the observations would have been made by night by means of reverberators or electric lamps.

On the first day, the two angles were measured, and the result inscribed on the double register ; and the astronomers all met in the evening at the camp which had been formed round the tree which had served for their point of sight. It was an immense baobab, more than 80 feet in circumference. Its syenite-coloured bark gave it a peculiar appearance. The whole caravan found room beneath its wide branches, which were inhabited by crowds of squirrels, which greedily devoured the white pulp of its egg-shaped fruit.

Supper was prepared for the Europeans by the ship's cook. There was no lack of venison, for the hunters had scoured the neighbourhood, and killed some antelopes ; and soon the air was filled with an odour of broiled meat, which still further aroused the appetite of the hungry savants.

After the comforting repast, the astronomers retired to their respective waggons, whilst Mokoum placed sentinels round the camp. Large fires of the dead branches of the baobab burnt throughout the night, and kept at a respectful distance the tawny beasts, who were attracted by the odour of the reeking flesh.

After two hours' sleep, however, Emery and Zorn got up, their observations not yet finished. They must find the altitudes of some stars to determine the latitude of the

Encampment under an immense Baobab.—[Page 74.]

station, and both, regardless of the day's fatigues, stood at their telescopes, and rigorously determined the change of zenith caused by the removal from the first station to the second, while the laugh of the hyena and the roar of the lion resounded over the sombre plain.

CHAPTER IX.

THE KRAAL.

THE next day operations were continued. The angle made by the baobab with the extremities of the base was measured, and the first triangle solved. Two more stations were chosen to the right and left of the meridian; one formed by a distinct mound, six miles away; the other, marked out by a post about seven miles distant.

The triangulation went on uninterruptedly for a month, and by the 15th of May the observers had advanced northwards 1°, having formed seven triangles. During this first series of operations, the Colonel and Strux were rarely together. The division of labour separated them, and the circumstance of their daily work being several miles apart was a guarantee against any dispute. Each evening they returned to their several abodes, and although at intervals discussions arose about the choice of stations, there was no serious altercation. Hence Zorn and his friend were in hopes that the survey would proceed without any open rupture.

After advancing 1° from the south, the observers found themselves in the same parallel with Lattakoo, from which they were distant 35 miles to the west.

Here a large kraal had lately been formed, and as it was a marked halting-place, Sir John Murray proposed that they should stay for several days. Zorn and Emery could take advantage of the rest, to take the altitude of the sun; and Palander would employ himself in reducing the measurements made at different points of sight to the uniform level of the sea. Sir John himself wanted to be free from scientific observations, that he might divert himself with his gun among the fauna of the country. A kraal, as it is termed by the natives of South Africa, is a kind of moving village, wandering from one pasturage to another. It is an enclosure composed ordinarily of about thirty habitations, and containing several hundred inhabitants. The kraal now reached was formed by a group of more than sixty huts, enclosed for protection from wild animals by a palisade of prickly aloes, and situated on the banks of a small affluent of the Kuruman. The huts, made of water-proof rush mats fastened to wooden beams, were like low hives. The doorway, protected by a skin, was so small that it could only be entered on hands and knees, and from this, the only aperture, issued such dense wreaths of smoke as would make existence in these abodes problematical to any but a Bochjesman or a Hottentot.

The whole population was roused by the arrival of the caravan. The dogs, of which there was one for the protection of each cabin, barked furiously, and about 200 warriors, armed with assagais, knives, and clubs, and protected by their leathern shields, marched forward.

A few words from Mokoum to one of the chiefs soon dispelled all hostile feeling, and the caravan obtained permission to encamp on the very banks of the stream. The Bochjesmen did not even refuse to share the pastures, which extended for miles away.

Mokoum having first given orders for the waggons to be placed in a circle as usual, mounted his zebra, and set off in company with Sir John Murray, who rode his accustomed horse. The hunters took their dogs and rifles, showing their intention of attacking the wild beasts, and went towards the woods.

"I hope, Mokoum," said Sir John, "that you are going to keep the promise you made at the Morgheda Falls, that you would bring me into the best sporting country in the world. But understand, I have not come here for hares or foxes; I can get them at home. Before another hour——"

"Hour!" replied the bushman. "You are rather too fast. A little patience, please. For myself, I am never patient except when hunting, and then I make amends for all my impatience at other times. Don't you know, Sir John, that the chase of large beasts is quite a science,

Here you must wait and watch. You must not step or even look too quickly. For my part, I have laid in wait for days together for a buffalo or gemsbok, and if I have had success at last, I have not considered my trouble in vain."

"Very good," replied Sir John, "I can show you as much patience as you can wish; but mind, the halt only lasts for three or four days, and we must lose no time."

"There is something in that," said the bushman, so calmly that Emery would not have recognized his companion of the Orange River; "we will just kill that which comes first, Sir John, antelope or deer, gnu or gazelle, any thing must do for hunters in a hurry."

"Antelope or gazelle!" cried Sir John, "why, what more could I ask, my good fellow?"

"As long as your honour is satisfied I have nothing more to say," said the bushman, somewhat ironically. "I thought that you would not let me off with any thing less than a rhinoceros or two, or at least an elephant."

"Any thing and any where," said Sir John, "we only waste time in talking."

The horses were put to a hand-gallop, and the hunters advanced quickly towards the forest. The plain rose with a gentle slope towards the north-east. It was dotted here and there with shrubs in full bloom, from which issued a viscous resin, transparent and odorous, of which the colonists

make a balm for wounds. In picturesque groups rose the
"nwanas," a kind of sycamore fig, whose trunks, leafless to
the height of 30 or 40 feet, supported a spreading parasol
of verdure. Among the foliage chattered swarms of scream-
ing parrots, eagerly pecking the sour figs. Farther on were
mimosas with their yellow clusters, "silver trees," shaking
their silky tufts, and aloes with spikes so red that they
might pass for coral plants torn from the depths of the sea.
The ground, enamelled with amaryllis with their bluish
foliage, was smooth and easy for the horses, and in less
than an hour after leaving the kraal, the sportsmen reached
the wood. For several miles extended a forest of acacias,
the entangled branches scarcely allowing a ray of sunlight
to penetrate to the ground below, which was encumbered
by brambles and long grass.

The hunters had little difficulty, however, in urging on
both horse and zebra, in spite of every obstacle, resting at
the recurring glades to examine the thickets around them.
The first day was not very favourable. In vain was the
forest scoured; not a single beast stirred, and Sir John's
thoughts turned more than once to the plains of Scotland,
where a shot is rarely long delayed. Mokoum evinced
neither surprise nor vexation; to him it was not a hunt, but
merely a rush across the forest.

Towards six in the evening they had to think about
returning. Sir John was more vexed than he would allow.

The Hunters. — [Page 80.]

Rather than that he, the renowned hunter, should return empty-handed, he resolved to shoot whatever first came within range, and fortune seemed to favour him.

They were not more than three miles from the kraal when a hare (of the species called "lepus rupestris") darted from a bush about 150 paces in front of them. Sir John did not hesitate a moment, and sent his explosive ball after the poor little animal.

The bushman gave a cry of indignation at such a ball being employed for such an aim; but the Englishman, eager for his prey, galloped to the spot where the victim fell. In vain! the only vestiges of the hare were the bloody morsels on the ground. Whilst the dogs rummaged in the brushwood, Sir John looked keenly about, and cried,—

"I am sure I hit it!"

"Rather too well," replied the bushman quietly.

And sure enough, the hare had been blown into countless fragments.

Sir John, greatly mortified, remounted his horse, and returned to camp, without uttering another word.

The next day the bushman waited for Sir John Murray to propose another expedition; but the Englishman applied himself for a time to his scientific instruments. For pastime he watched the occupants of the kraal as they practised with their bows, or played on the "gorah," an instrument composed of a piece of catgut stretched on a bow, and kept in vibration by blowing through an ostrich feather. He remarked that the women, while occupied in their domestic duties, smoked "matokouané," that is, the unwholesome hemp-plant, a practice indulged in by most of the natives. According to some travellers, this inhaling of hemp increases physical strength to the damage of mental energy; and, indeed, many of the Bochjesmen appeared stupefied from its effects.

At dawn, however, the following day, Sir John Murray was aroused by the appearance of Mokoum, who said, "I think, sir, we may be fortunate enough to-day to find something better than a hare."

Sir John, not heeding the satire, declared himself ready; and the two hunters, accordingly, were off betimes. This time, Sir John, instead of his formidable rifle, carried a simple gun of Goldwin's, as being a more suitable weapon. True, there was a chance of meeting some prowling beast from the forest; but he had the hare on his mind, and would sooner use small shot against a lion than repeat an incident unprecedented in the annals of sport.

Fortune, to-day, was more favourable to the hunters. They brought down a couple of harrisbucks, a rare kind of black antelope, very difficult to shoot. These were charming animals, four feet high, with long diverging horns shaped like scimitars. The tips of their noses were narrow; they had black hoofs, close soft hair, and pointed ears. Their face and belly, white as snow, contrasted well with their black back, over which fell a wavy mane. Hunters may well be proud of such shots, for the harrisbuck has always been the *desideratum* of the Delegorgues, Vahlbergs, Cummings, and Baldwins, and it is one of the finest specimens of the southern fauna.

But what made the Englishman's heart beat fastest, was Mokoum's showing him certain marks on the edge of the thick underwood, not far from a deep pool, surrounded by giant euphorbias, and whose surface was dotted with sky-blue water-lilies.

"Come and lie in ambush here to-morrow, sir," said Mokoum, "and this time you may bring your rifle. Look at these fresh footprints."

"What are they? Can they be an elephant's?" asked Sir John.

"Yes," replied Mokoum, "and, unless I am mistaken, of a male full-grown."

Eagerly, then, was the engagement made for the following day. Sir John's horse, as they returned, carried the harrisbucks. These fine creatures, so rarely captured, excited the admiration of the whole caravan, and all congratulated Sir John, except perhaps Matthew Strux, who knew little of animals, except the Great Bear, the Centaur, Pegasus, and other celestial fauna.

At four o'clock the next morning, the hunters, attended

by their dogs, were already hidden in the underwood. They had discovered by new footmarks that the elephants came in a troop to drink at the pool. Their grooved rifles carried explosive bullets. Silent and still, they watched for about half-an-hour, when they observed a movement in the grove, about fifty paces from the pool. Sir John seized his gun, but the bushman made him a sign to restrain his impatience. Soon large shadows appeared: the thickets rustled under the violence of some pressure; the brushwood snapped and crackled, and the sound of a loud breathing was perceptible through the branches. It was the herd of elephants. Half-a-dozen gigantic creatures, almost as large as those of India, advanced slowly towards the pool. The increasing daylight allowed Sir John, struck with admiration, to notice especially a male of enormous size. His colossal proportions appeared in the partial light even greater than they really were. While his trunk was extended above the underwood, with his curved tusks he struck the great stems, which groaned under the shock. The bushman leant down close to Sir John's ear, and whispered,—

"Will he suit you?"

Sir John made a sign of affirmation.

"Then," said Mokoum, "we will separate him from the rest."

At this instant, the elephants reached the edge of the pool, and their spongy feet sank into the soft mud. They pumped up the water with their trunks, and poured it into their throats with a loud gurgling. The great male looked uneasily about him, and seemed to scent some approaching danger.

Suddenly the bushman gave a peculiar cry. The dogs, barking furiously, darted from concealment, and rushed towards the herd. At the same moment, Mokoum, charging his companion to remain where he was, went off on his zebra to intercept the elephant's retreat. The animal made no attempt to take flight, and Sir John, with his finger on the lock of his rifle, watched him closely. The brute beat the trees, and lashed his tail furiously, showing signs not of uneasiness, but of anger. Now, for the first time, catching sight of his enemy, he rushed upon him at once.

Sir John was about sixty paces distant; and waiting till the elephant came within forty paces, he aimed at his flank and fired. But a movement of the horse made his aim unsteady, and the ball only entered the soft flesh without meeting any obstacle sufficient to make it explode.

The enraged beast increased its pace, which was rather a rapid walk than a run, and would have soon distanced the horse. Sir John's horse reared, and rushed from the thicket, his master unable to hold him in. The elephant followed, ears erect, and bellowing like a trumpet. Sir John, thus carried away, held on to his horse tightly with his knees, and endeavoured to slip a cartridge into the chamber of his rifle. Still the elephant gained on him. They were soon beyond the wood, and out on the plain. Sir John vigorously used his spurs, and the two dogs rushed panting in the rear. The elephant was not two lengths behind. Sir John could hear the hissing of his trunk, and almost feel his strong breath. Every moment he expected to be dragged from his saddle by the living lasso. All at once the horse sunk on his hind-quarters, struck by the elephant on his haunches. He neighed, and sprung to one side, thus saving Sir John. The elephant, unable to check his course, passed on, and sweeping the ground with his trunk, caught up one of the dogs, and shook it in the air with tremendous violence. No resource remained except to re-enter the wood, and the horse's instinct carried him thither. The elephant continued to give chase, brandishing the unlucky dog, whose head he smashed against a sycamore as he rushed into the forest. The horse darted into a dense thicket entangled with prickly creepers, and stopped.

Sir John, torn and bleeding, but not for an instant discomposed, turned round, and shouldering his rifle, took aim at the elephant close to the shoulder, through the net-work of creepers. The ball exploded as it struck the bone. The animal staggered, and almost at the same moment a second shot from the edge of the wood struck his left flank. He fell on his knees near a little pool, half-hidden in the grass. There, pumping up the water with his

The Elephant and the Dog.—[Page 86.]

"He is ours! he is ours!"—[Page 87.]

trunk, he began to wash his wounds, uttering plaintive cries. The bushman now appeared, shouting, "He is ours, he is ours!"

And in truth the animal was mortally wounded. He groaned piteously, and breathed hard. His tail moved feebly, and his trunk, fed from the pool of his blood, poured back a crimson stream on the surrounding brushwood. Gradually failed his strength, and the great beast was dead.

Sir John Murray now emerged from the grove. He was half naked, little of his hunting costume remaining but rags. But he felt as though he could have given his very skin for this triumph.

"A glorious fellow!" he exclaimed, as he examined the carcase; "but rather too big to carry home."

"True, sir," answered Mokoum; "we will cut him up on the spot, and carry off the choice parts. Look at his magnificent tusks! Twenty-five pounds a-piece at least! And ivory at five shillings a-pound will mount up."

Thus talking, the hunter proceeded to cut up the animal. He took off the tusks with his hatchet, and contented himself with the feet and trunk, as choice morsels with which to regale the members of the Commission. This operation took some time, and he and his companion did not get back to camp before midday. The bushman had the elephant's feet cooked according to the African method, that is, by burying them in a hole previously heated, like an oven, with hot coals.

The delicacy was fully appreciated by all, not excepting the phlegmatic Palander, and Sir John Murray received a hearty round of compliments.

CHAPTER X.

THE RAPID.

DURING their sojourn by the kraal, Colonel Everest and Matthew Strux had been absolutely strangers. On the eve of their departure for their divided labours, they had ceremoniously taken leave one of the other, and had not since met. The caravan continued its northward route, and the weather being favourable, during the next ten days two fresh triangles were measured. The vast verdant wilderness was intersected by streams flowing between rows of the willow-like "karree-hout," from which the Bochjesmen make their bows. Large tracts of desert land occurred, where every trace of moisture disappeared, leaving the soil utterly bare but for the cropping-up occasionally of those mucilaginous plants which no aridity can kill. For miles there was no natural object that could be used for a station, and consequently the astronomers were obliged to employ natural objects for their point of sight. This caused considerable loss of time, but was not attended with much real difficulty. The crew of the "Queen and Czar" were employed in this part of the work, and performed their task well and rapidly; but the same jealousy that divided their chiefs crept in sometimes among the seamen. Zorn and Emery did all they could to neutralize any unpleasantness, but the discussions sometimes took a serious character. The Colonel and Strux continually interfered in behalf of their countrymen, whether they were right or wrong, but they only succeeded in making matters worse. After a while Zorn and Emery were the only members of the party who had preserved a perfect concord. Even Sir John Murray and Nicholas Palander (generally absorbed as they were, the one in his calculations, the other in his hunting), began to join the fray.

One day the dispute went so far that Strux said to the Colonel, "You must please to moderate your tone with astronomers from Poulkowa: remember it was their telescope that showed that the disc of Uranus is circular."

"Yes," replied the Colonel; "but ours at Cambridge enabled us to classify the nebula of Andromeda."

The irritation was evident, and at times seemed to imperil the fate of the triangulation. Hitherto the discussions had had no injurious effect, but perhaps rather served to keep every operation more scrupulously exact.

On the 30th the weather suddenly changed. In any other region a storm and torrents of rain might have been expected: angry-looking clouds covered the sky, and lightning, unaccompanied by thunder, gleamed through the mass of vapour. But condensation did not ensue—not a drop of rain fell on to the thirsty soil. The sky remained overcast for some days, and the fog rendered the points of sight invisible at the distance of a mile. The astronomers, however, would not lose time, and determined to set up lighted signals and work at night. The bushman prudently advised caution, lest the electric lights should attract the wild beasts too closely to their quarters; and in fact, during the night, the yelp of the jackal and the hoarse laugh of the hyena, like that of a drunken negro, could plainly be heard.

In the midst of this clamour, in which the roar of a lion could sometimes be distinguished, the astronomers felt rather distracted, and the measurements were taken at least less rapidly, if not less accurately. To take zenith distances while gleaming eyes might be gazing at them through the darkness, required imperturbable composure and the utmost *sang-froid*. But these qualities were not wanting in the members of the Commission, and after a few days they regained their presence of mind, and worked away in the midst of the beasts as calmly as if they were in their own observatories. Armed hunters attended them at every station, and no inconsiderable number of hyenas fell by their balls. Sir John thought this way of surveying delightful, and whilst his eye was at his telescope his hand was on his gun, and more than once he made a shot in the interval between two observations.

Nothing occurred to check the steady progress of the survey, so that the astronomers hoped before the end of June to measure a second degree of the meridian. On the 17th they found that their path was crossed by an affluent of the Kuruman. The Europeans could easily take their instruments across in their india-rubber canoe ; but Mokoum would have to take the caravan to a ford which he remembered some miles below. The river was about half-a-mile wide, and its rapid current, broken here and there by rocks and stems of trees embedded in the mud, offered considerable danger to any light craft. Matthew Strux did not fail to represent this, but finding that his companions did not recoil from the attempt he gave way.

Nicholas Palander alone was to accompany the caravan in its *détour*. He was too much absorbed in his calculations to give any thought to danger ; but his presence was not indispensable to his companions, and the boat would only hold a limited number of passengers. Accordingly, he gave up his place to an Englishman of the crew of the "Queen and Czar," who would be more useful under the circumstances.

After making an arrangement to meet to the north of the rapid, the caravan disappeared down the left bank of the stream, leaving Colonel Everest, Strux, Emery, Zorn, Sir John, two sailors, and a Bochjesman, who was the pioneer of the caravan, and had been recommended by Mokoum as having much experience in African rapids.

"A pretty river," observed Zorn to his friend, as the sailors were preparing the boat.

"Very so, but hard to cross," answered Emery. "These rapids have not long to live, and therefore enjoy life. With a few weeks of this dry season there will hardly remain enough of this swollen torrent to water a caravan. It is soon exhausted; such is the law of nature, moral and physical. But we must not waste time in moralizing. See, the boat is equipped, and I am all anxiety to see her performances."

In a few minutes the boat was launched beside a sloping bank of red granite. Here, sheltered by a projecting rock, the water quietly bathed the reeds and creepers. The instruments and provisions were put in the boat, and the passengers seated themselves so as not to interfere with the action of the oars. The Bochjesman took the helm; he spoke but a few words of English, and advised the travellers to keep a profound silence while they were crossing. The boat soon felt the influence of the current. The sailors carefully obeyed every order of the Bochjesman. Sometimes they had to raise their oars to avoid some half-emerged stump; sometimes to row hard across a whirlpool.

When the current became too strong they could only guide the light boat as it drifted with the stream. The native, tiller in hand, sat watchful and motionless, prepared for every danger. The Europeans were half uneasy at their novel situation; they seemed carried away by an irresistible force. The Colonel and Strux gazed at each other without a word; Sir John, with his rifle between his knees, watched the numerous birds that skimmed the water; and the two younger astronomers gazed with admiration at the banks, past which they flew with dizzy speed. The light boat soon reached the true rapid, which it was necessary to cross obliquely. At a word from the Bochjesman, the sailors put forth their strength; but, despite all their efforts, they were carried down parallel to the banks. The tiller and oars had no longer any effect, and the situation became really perilous; a rock or stump of a tree would inevitably have overturned the boat. In spite of the manifest peril, no one uttered a word. The Bochjesman half rose, and watched the direction which he could not control. Two hundred yards distant rose an islet of stones and trees, which it was impossible to avoid. In a few seconds the boat apparently must be lost; but the shock came with less violence than had seemed inevitable. The boat lurched and shipped a little water, but the passengers kept their places. They were astonished to observe that what they had presumed to be rock had moved, and was plunging

The Hippopotamus did not quit his hold, but shook the Boat as a Dog would a Hare.—[Page 95.]

about in the rush of the waters. It was an immense hippopotamus, ten feet long, which had been carried by the current against the islet, and dared not venture out again into the rapid. Feeling the shock, he raised and shook his head, looking about him with his little dull eyes, and with his mouth wide open, showing his great canine teeth. He rushed furiously on the boat, which he threatened to bite to pieces.

But Sir John Murray's presence of mind did not forsake him. Quietly shouldering his rifle, he fired at the animal near the ear. The hippopotamus did not quit his hold, but shook the boat as a dog would a hare. A second shot was soon lodged in his head. The blow was mortal. After pushing the boat with a last effort off the islet, the fleshy mass sank in the deep water. Before the dismayed voyagers could collect their thoughts, they were whirled obliquely into the rapid. A hundred yards below, a sharp bend in the river broke the current; thither was the boat carried, and was arrested by a violent shock. Safe and sound the whole party leapt to the bank. They were about two miles below the spot where they had embarked.

CHAPTER XI.

A MISSING COMPANION.

IN continuing the survey the astronomers had to be on their guard against the serpents that infested the region, venomous mambas, ten to twelve feet long, whose bite would have been fatal.

Four days after the passage of the rapid, the observers found themselves in a wooded country. The trees, however, were not so high as to interfere with their labours, and at all points rose eminences which afforded excellent sites for the posts and electric lamps. The district, lying considerably lower than the rest of the plain, was moist and fertile. Emery noticed thousands of Hottentot fig-trees, whose sour fruit is much relished by the Bochjesmen. From the ground arose a soft odour from the "kucumakranti," a yellow fruit two or three inches long, growing from bulbous roots like the colchicum, and eagerly devoured by the native children. Here, too, in this more watered country, reappeared the fields of colocynths and borders of the mint so successfully naturalized in England. Notwithstanding its fertility, the country appeared little frequented by the wandering tribes, and not a kraal or a camp-fire was to be seen; yet water was abundant, forming some considerable streams and lagoons.

The astronomers halted to await the caravan. The time fixed by Mokoum had just expired, and if he had reckoned well, he would join them to-day. The day, however, passed on, and no Bochjesman appeared. Sir John conjectured that the hunter had probably been obliged to ford farther south than he had expected, since the river was unusually swollen. Another day passed and the caravan had not appeared. The Colonel became uneasy; he could not go on, and the delay might affect the success of the operations. Matthew Strux said that it had always been his wish to accompany the caravan, and that if his advice had been followed they would not have found themselves in this predicament; but he would not admit that the responsibility rested on the Russians. Colonel Everest began to protest against these insinuations, but Sir John interposed, saying that what was done could not be undone, and that all the recriminations in the world would make no difference.

It was then decided that if the caravan did not appear on the following day, Emery and Zorn, under the guidance of the Bochjesman, should start to ascertain the reason of the

H

delay. For the rest of the day the rivals kept apart, and Sir John passed his time in beating the surrounding woods. He failed in finding any game, but from a naturalist's point of view he ought to have been satisfied, since he brought down two fine specimens of African birds. One was a kind of partridge, a francolin, thirteen inches long, with short legs, dark grey back, red beak and claws, and elegant wings, shaded with brown. The other bird, with a red throat and white tail, was a species of falcon. The Bochjesman pioneer cleverly took off the skins, in order that they should be preserved entire.

The next day was half over, and the two young men were just about to start on their search, when a distant bark arrested them. Soon Mokoum, on his zebra, emerged at full speed from the thicket of aloes on the left, and advanced towards the camp.

"Welcome," cried Sir John joyfully, "we had almost given you up, and apart from you I should be inconsolable. I am only successful when you are with me. We will celebrate your return in a glass of usquebaugh."

Mokoum made no answer, but anxiously scanned and counted the Europeans. Colonel Everest perceived his perplexity, and as he was dismounting, said,—

"For whom are you looking, Mokoum?"

"For Mr. Palander," replied the bushman.

"Is he not with you?" said the Colonel.

"Not now," answered Mokoum. "I thought I should find him with you. He is lost!"

At these words, Matthew Strux stepped forward.

"Lost!" he cried. "He was confided to your care. You are responsible for his safety, and it is not enough to say he is lost."

Mokoum's face flushed, and he answered impatiently,—

"Why should you expect me to take care of one who can't take care of himself? Why blame me? If Mr. Palander is lost, it is by his own folly. Twenty times I have found him absorbed in his figures, and have brought him back to the caravan. But the evening before last he disappeared, and I have not seen him since. Perhaps if you are so clever, you can spy him out with your telescope."

The bushman would doubtless have become more irritable still, if Sir John had not pacified him. Matthew Strux had not been able to get in a word, but now turned round unexpectedly to the Colonel, saying,—

"I shall not abandon my countryman. I suppose that if Sir John Murray or Mr. Emery were lost, you would suspend operations; and I don't see why you should do less for a Russian than for an Englishman."

"Mr. Strux," cried the Colonel, folding his arms, and fixing his eyes on his adversary, "do you wish to insult me? Why should you suppose that we will not seek this blundering calculator?"

"Sir!" said Strux.

"Yes, blundering," repeated the Colonel. "And to return to what you said, I maintain that any embarrassment to the progress of the operations from this circumstance would be due to the Russians alone."

"Colonel," cried Strux, with gleaming eyes, "your words are hasty."

"My words, on the contrary, are well weighed. Let it be understood that operations are suspended until Mr. Palander is found. Are you ready to start?"

"I was ready before you spoke a word," answered Strux sharply.

The caravan having now arrived, the disputants each went to his waggon. On the way Sir John could not help saying,—

"It is lucky that the stupid fellow has not carried off the double register."

"Just what I was thinking," said the Colonel.

The Englishmen proceeded more strictly to interrogate Mokoum. He told them that Palander had been missing for two days, and had last been seen alongside of the caravan about twelve miles from the encampment; that after missing him, he at once set out to seek for him, but being unsuccessful in all his search, had concluded that he must have made his way to his companions.

Mokoum proposed that they should now explore the

woods to the north-east, adding that they must not lose an hour if they wanted to find him alive, knowing that no one could wander with impunity for two days in a country infested like that with wild beasts. Where any one else could find a subsistence, Palander, ever engrossed by his figures, would inevitably die of starvation. At one o'clock, guided by the hunter, they mounted and left the camp. The grotesque attitudes of Strux, as he clung uneasily to his steed, caused considerable diversion to his companions, who, however, were polite enough to pass no remark.

Before leaving the camp, Mokoum asked the pioneer to lend him his keen-scented dog. The sagacious animal, after scenting a hat belonging to Palander, darted off in a north-easterly direction, whilst his master urged him on by a peculiar whistle. The little troop followed, and soon disappeared in the underwood.

All the day the Colonel and his companions followed the dog, who seemed instinctively to know what was required of him. They shouted, they fired their guns, but night came on when they had scoured the woods for five miles round, and they were at length obliged to rest until the following day. They spent the night in a grove, before which the bushman had prudently kindled a wood fire. Some wild howls were heard, by no means reassuring. Hours passed in arguing about Palander, and discussing plans for his assistance. The English showed as much devotion as Strux could desire; and it was decided that all work should be adjourned till the Russian was found, alive or dead.

After a weary night the day dawned. The horses were saddled, and the little troop again followed the dog. Towards the north-east they arrived at a district almost swampy in its character. The small water-courses increased in number, but they were easily forded, care being taken to avoid the crocodiles, of which Sir John, for the first time in his life, now saw some specimens. The bushman would not permit that time should be wasted in any attack upon the reptiles, and restrained Sir John, who was always on the *qui-vive* to discharge a ball. Whenever a crocodile, snapping its prey with its formidable jaw, put its head out of water, the horses set off at a gallop to escape.

The troop of riders went on over woods, plains, and marshes, noting the most insignificant tokens: here a broken bough; there a freshly-trodden tuft of grass; or farther on some inexplicable mark; but no trace of Palander.

When they had advanced ten miles north of the last encampment, and were about to turn south-east, the dog suddenly gave signs of agitation. He barked, and in an excited way wagged his tail. Sniffing the dry grass, he ran on a few steps, and returned to the same spot.

"The dog scents something," exclaimed the bushman.

"It seems," said Sir John, "he is on a right track.

"There he is," cried Mokoum.—[Page 103.]

Listen to his yelping: he seems to be talking to himself. He will be an invaluable creature if he scents out Palander."

Strux did not quite relish the way in which his countryman was treated as a head of game; but the important thing now was to find him, and they all waited to follow the dog, as soon as he should be sure of the scent.

Very soon the animal, with a loud yelp, bounded over the thicket and disappeared. The horses could not follow through the dense forest, but were obliged to take a circuitous path. The dog was certainly on the right track now, the only question was whether Palander was alive or dead.

In a few minutes the yelping ceased, and the bushman and Sir John, who were in advance, were becoming uneasy, when suddenly the barking began again outside the forest, about half a mile away. The horses were spurred in that direction, and soon reached the confines of the marsh. The dog could distinctly be heard, but, on account of the lofty reeds, could not be seen. The riders dismounted, and tied their horses to a tree. With difficulty they made their way through the reeds, and reached a large space covered with water and aquatic plants. In the lowest part lay the brown waters of a lagoon half a mile square. The dog stopped at the muddy edge, and barked furiously.

"There he is!" cried Mokoum.

And sure enough, on a stump at the extremity of a sort of peninsula, sat Nicholas Palander, pencil in hand, and a note-book on his knees, wrapt in calculations. His friends could not suppress a cry. About twenty paces off a number of crocodiles, quite unknown to him, lay watching, and evidently designing an attack.

"Make haste," said Mokoum, in a low voice; "I don't understand why these animals don't rush on him."

"They are waiting till he is gamey," said Sir John, alluding to the idea common among the natives that these reptiles never touch fresh meat.

The bushman and Sir John, telling their companions to wait for them, passed round the lagoon, and reached the narrow isthmus by which alone they could get near Palander. They had not gone two hundred steps, when the crocodiles, leaving the water, made straight towards their prey. Palander saw nothing, but went on writing.

"Be quick and calm," whispered Mokoum, "or all is lost."

Both, kneeling down, aimed at the nearest reptiles, and fired. Two monsters rolled into the water with broken backs, and the rest simultaneously disappeared beneath the surface.

At the sound of the guns Palander raised his head. He recognized his companions, and ran towards them waving

A missing Companion.—[Page 104.]

his note-book, and like the philosopher of old exclaiming "Eureka!" he cried, "I have found it!"

"What have you found?" asked Sir John.

"An error in the last decimal of a logarithm of James Wolston's."

It was a fact. The worthy man had discovered the error, and had secured a right to the prize offered by Wolston's editor. For four days had the astronomer wandered in solitude. Truly Ampère, with his unrivalled gift of abstraction, could not have done better!

CHAPTER XII.

A STATION TO SIR JOHN'S LIKING.

So the Russian mathematician was found! When they asked him how he had passed those four days, he could not tell; he thought the whole story of the crocodiles was a joke, and did not believe it. He had not been hungry; he had lived upon figures. Matthew Strux would not reproach his countryman before his colleagues, but there was every reason to believe that in private he gave him a severe reprimand.

The geodetic operations were now resumed, and went on as usual till the 28th of June, when they had measured the base of the 15th triangle, which would conclude the second and commence the third degree of the meridian. Here a physical difficulty arose. The country was so thickly covered with underwood, that although the artificial signals could be erected, they could not be discerned at any distance. One station was recognized as available for an electric lamp. This was a mountain 1200 feet high, about thirty miles to the north-west. The choice of this would make the sides of this triangle considerably longer than any of the former, but it was at length determined to adopt it. Colonel Everest, Emery, Zorn, three sailors, and two Bochjesmen, were appointed to establish the lighted signal, the distance being too great to work otherwise than at night.

The little troop, accompanied by mules laden with the instruments and provisions, set off in the morning. The Colonel did not expect to reach the base of the mountain till the following day, and however few might be the difficulties of the ascent, the observers in the camp would not see the lighted signal till the night of the 29th or 30th.

In the interval of waiting, Strux and Palander went to their usual occupations, while Sir John and the bushman shot antelopes. They found opportunity of hunting a giraffe, which is considered fine sport. Coming across a herd of twenty, but so wild that they could not approach within 500 yards, they succeeded in detaching a female from the herd. The animal set off at first at a slow trot, allowing the horsemen to gain upon her; but when she found them near, she twisted her tail, and started at full speed. The hunters followed for about two miles, when a ball from Sir John's rifle threw her on to her side, and made her an easy victim.

In the course of the next night the two Russians took some altitudes of the stars, which enabled them to determine the latitude of the encampment. The following night was clear and dry, without moon and stars, and the observers impatiently watched for the appearance of the electric light. Strux, Palander, and Sir John relieved guard at the telescope, but no light appeared. They concluded that the ascent of the mountain had offered serious difficulty, and again postponed their observations till the next night. Great, however, was their surprise, when, about two o'clock in the afternoon, Colonel Everest and his companions suddenly reappeared in camp.

In answer to inquiries whether he had found the mountain inaccessible, Colonel Everest replied that although in itself the mountain was entirely accessible, it was so guarded that they had found it necessary to come back for reinforcements.

"Do you mean," said Sir John, "that the natives were assembled in force?"

"Yes, natives with four paws and black manes, who have eaten up one of our horses."

The Colonel went on to say that the mountain was only to be approached by a spur on the south-west side. In the narrow defile leading to the spur a troop of lions had taken up their abode. These he had endeavoured to dislodge, but, insufficiently armed, he was compelled to beat a retreat, after losing one of his horses by a single blow of a lion's paw.

The recital kindled the interest of Sir John and the bushman. Clearly it was a station worth conquering, and an expedition was at once arranged. All the Europeans, without exception, were eager to join, but it was necessary that some should remain at the camp to measure the angles at the base of the triangle, therefore the Colonel resolved to stay behind with Strux and Palander, while Sir John, Emery, and Zorn (to whose entreaties their chiefs had been obliged to yield), Mokoum, and three natives on whose courage he could rely, made up the party for the attack.

They started at four in the afternoon, and by nine were within two miles of the mountain. Here they dismounted, and made their arrangements for the night. No fire was kindled, Mokoum being unwilling to provoke a nocturnal attack from the animals, which he wished to meet by daylight.

Throughout the night the roar of the lions could almost incessantly be heard. Not one of the hunters slept for so much as an hour, and Mokoum took advantage of their wakefulness to give them some advice from his own experience.

"From what Colonel Everest tells us," he said calmly, "these are black-maned lions, the fiercest and most dangerous species of any. They leap for a distance of sixteen to twenty paces, and I should advise you to avoid their first bound. Should the first fail, they rarely take a second. We will attack them as they re-enter their den at daybreak; they are always less fierce when they are well filled. But they will defend themselves well, for here, in this uninhabited district, they are unusually ferocious. Measure your distance well before you fire; let the animal approach, and take a sure aim near the shoulder. We must leave our horses behind; the sight of a lion terrifies them, and therefore the safety of their rider is imperilled. We must fight on foot, and I rely on your calmness."

All listened with silent attention: Mokoum was now the patient hunter. Although the lion seldom attacks a man without provocation, yet his fury, when once aroused, is terrible; and therefore the bushman enjoined composure on his companions, especially on Sir John, who was often carried away by his boldness.

"Shoot at a lion," said Mokoum, "as calmly as if you were shooting a partridge."

At four o'clock, only a few red streaks being visible in the far east, the hunters tied up their horses securely and left their halting-place.

"Examine your guns, and be careful that your cartridges are in good trim," continued Mokoum, to those who carried rifles; for the three natives were armed otherwise, satisfied with their bows of aloe, which already had rendered them good service.

The party, in a compact group, turned towards the defile, which had been partially reconnoitred the evening before.

They crept, like Red Indians, silently between the trees, and soon reached the narrow gorge which formed the entrance. Here, winding between piles of granite, began the path leading to the first slopes of the spur. Midway the path had been widened by a landslip, and here was the cave tenanted by the lions.

It was then arranged that Sir John, one of the natives, and Mokoum, should creep along the upper edge of the defile, with the intention of driving out the animals to the lower extremity of the gorge. There the two young Europeans and the other two Bochjesmen should be in ambush to receive the fugitive beasts with shot and arrows.

No spot could be better adapted for the manœuvres. The forked branches of a gigantic sycamore afforded a safe position, since lions do not climb; and the hunters, perched at a considerable height, could escape their bounds and aim at them under favourable conditions.

William Emery objected to the plan as being dangerous for Sir John and the bushman, but the latter would hear of no modification, and Emery reluctantly acquiesced.

Day now began to dawn, and the mountain-top was glowing in the sun. Mokoum, after seeing his four companions installed in the sycamore, started off with Sir John and the Bochjesman, and soon mounted the devious path which lay on the right edge of the defile. Cautiously examining their path, they continued to advance. In the event of the lions having returned to their den and being at repose, it would be possible to make short work of them.

After about a quarter of an hour the hunters, reaching the landslip before the cave to which Zorn had directed them, crouched down and examined the spot. It seemed a wide excavation, though at present they could hardly estimate the size. The entrance was marked by piles of bones and remains of animals, demonstrating, beyond doubt, that it was the lions' retreat.

Contrary to the hunter's expectation, the cave seemed deserted. He crept to the entrance and satisfied himself that it was really empty. Calling his companions, who joined him immediately, he said,—

" Our game has not returned, Sir John, but it will not be long : I think we had better install ourselves in its place. Better to be besieged than besiegers, especially as we have an armed succour at hand. What do you think ?"

" I am at your orders, Mokoum," replied Sir John.

All three accordingly entered. It was a deep grotto, strewn with bones and stained with blood. Repeating their scrutiny, lest they should be mistaken as to the cave being empty, they hastened to barricade the entrance by piling up stones, the intervening spaces being filled with boughs and dry brushwood. This only occupied a few

It was a deep Grotto, strewn with Bones and stained with Blood.—[Page 112.]

The Entrance to the Lion's Den.—[Page 112.]

minutes, the mouth of the cave being comparatively narrow. They then went behind their loop-holes, and awaited their prey, which was not long in coming. A lion and two lionesses approached within a hundred yards of the cave. The lion, tossing his mane and sweeping the ground with his tail, carried in his teeth an entire antelope, which he shook with as much ease as a cat would a mouse. The two lionesses frisked along at his side.

Sir John afterwards confessed that it was a moment of no little trepidation; he felt his pulses beat fast, and was conscious of something like fear; but he was soon himself again. His two companions retained their composure undisturbed.

At the sight of the barricade, the beasts paused. They were within sixty paces. With a harsh roar from the lion, they all three rushed into a thicket on the right, a little below the spot where the hunters had first stopped. Their tawny backs and gleaming eyes were distinctly visible through the foliage.

"The partridges are there," whispered Sir John; "let us each take one."

"No," answered Mokoum softly, "the brood is not all here, and the report of a gun would frighten the rest. Bochjesman, are you sure of your arrow at this distance?"

"Yes, Mokoum," said the native.

"Then aim at the male's left flank, and pierce his heart."

The Bochjesman bent his bow, and the arrow whistled through the brushwood. With a loud roar, the lion made a bound and fell. He lay motionless, and his sharp teeth stood out in strong relief against his blood-stained lips.

"Well done, Bochjesman!" said Mokoum.

At this moment the lionesses, leaving the thicket, flung themselves on the lion's body. Attracted by their roar, two other lions and a third lioness appeared round the corner of the defile. Bristling with anger, they looked twice their ordinary size, and bounded forward with terrific roars.

"Now for the rifles," cried the bushman, "we must shoot them on the wing, since they will not perch."

The bushman took deliberate aim, and one lion fell, as it were paralyzed. The other, his paw broken by Sir John's bullet, rushed towards the barricade, followed by the infuriated lionesses. Unless the rifles could now be brought successfully to bear, the three animals would succeed in entering their den. The hunters retired; their guns were quickly reloaded; two or three lucky shots, and all would be well; but an unforeseen circumstance occurred which rendered the hunters' situation to the last degree alarming.

All at once a dense smoke filled the cave. One of the wads, falling on the dry brushwood, had set it alight, and soon a sheet of flames, fanned by the wind, lay between the

A Ball from the Bushman arrested the Lioness.—[Page 115.]

men and the beasts. The lions recoiled, but the hunters would be suffocated if they remained where they were. It was a terrible moment, but they dared not hesitate.

"Come out! come out!" cried Mokoum.

They pushed aside the brushwood with the butt ends of their guns, knocked down the stones, and, half choked, leaped out of the cloud of smoke.

The native and Sir John had hardly time to collect their senses when they were both knocked over. The African, struck on the chest by one of the lionesses, lay motionless on the ground; Sir John, who received a blow from the tail of the other, thought his leg was broken, and fell on his knees. But just as the animal turned upon him, a ball from the bushman arrested her, and, meeting a bone, exploded in her body. At this instant Zorn, Emery, and the two Bochjesmen appeared opportunely, although unsummoned, hastening up the defile. Two lions and one lioness were dead; but two lionesses and the lion with the broken paw were still sufficiently formidable. The rifles, however, performed their duty. A second lioness fell, struck in both head and flank. The third lioness and the wounded lion bounded over the young men's heads, and amid a last salute of balls and arrows disappeared round the corner of the defile.

Sir John uttered a loud hurrah. The lions were conquered, four carcasses measured the ground.

With his friend's assistance, Sir John was soon on his feet again; his leg was not broken. The native soon recovered his consciousness, being merely stunned by the blow from the animal's head. An hour later, the little troop, without further trace of the fugitive couple, regained the thicket where they had left their horses.

"Well," said Mokoum to Sir John, "I hope you like our African partridges."

"Delightful! delightful!" said Sir John, rubbing his leg, "but what tails they have, to be sure!"

" Well," said Mokoum, " I hope you like our African Partridges."—[Page 116.]

CHAPTER XIII.

PACIFICATION BY FIRE.

AT the camp Colonel Everest and his colleagues, with a natural impatience, anxiously abided the result of the lion-hunt. If the chase proved successful, the light would appear in the course of the night. The Colonel and Strux passed the day uneasily; Palander, always engrossed, forgot that any danger menaced his friends. It might be said of him, as of the mathematician Bouvard, "He will continue to calculate while he continues to live;" for apart from his calculations life for him would have lost its purpose.

The two chiefs certainly thought quite as much of the accomplishment of their survey as of any danger incurred by their companions; they would themselves have braved any peril rather than have a physical obstacle to arrest their operations.

At length, after a day that seemed interminable, the night arrived. Punctually every half-hour the Colonel and

Matthew Strux silently relieved guard at the telescope, each desiring to be the first to discover the light. But hours passed on, and no light appeared. At last, at a quarter to three, Colonel Everest arose, and calmly said. "The signal!"

The Russian, although he did not utter a word, could scarcely conceal the chagrin which he felt at chance favouring the Colonel.

The angle was then carefully measured, and was found to be exactly $73° 58' 42''.413$.

Colonel Everest being anxious to join his companions as soon as possible, the camp was raised at dawn, and by midday all the members of the Commission had met once more. The incidents of the lion-hunt were recounted, and the victors heartily congratulated.

During the morning Sir John, Emery, and Zorn had proceeded to the summit of the mountain, and had thence measured the angular distance of a new station situated a few miles to the west of the meridian. Palander also announced that the measurement of the second degree was now complete.

For five weeks all went on well. The weather was fine, and the country, being only slightly undulated, offered fair sites for the stations. Provisions were abundant, and Sir John's revictualling expeditions provided full many a variety of antelopes and buffaloes. The general health was good, and water could always be found. Even the discussions between the Colonel and Strux were less violent, and each seemed to vie with the other in zeal for success, when a local difficulty occurred which for a while hindered the work and revived hostilities.

It was the 11th of August. During the night the caravan had passed through a wooded country, and in the morning halted before an immense forest extending beyond the horizon. Imposing masses of foliage formed a verdant curtain which was of indescribable beauty. There were the "gounda," the "mosokoso," and the "mokoumdon," a wood much sought for ship-building; great ebony trees, their bark covering a perfectly black wood; "bauhinias," with fibre of iron; "buchneras," with their orange-coloured flowers; magnificent "roodeblatts," with whitish trunks, crowned with crimson foliage, and thousands of "guaiacums," measuring fifteen feet in circumference. There was ever a murmur like that of the surf on a sandy coast; it was the wind, which, passing across the branches, was calmed on the skirts of the forest. In answer to a question from the Colonel, Mokoum said,—

" It is the forest of Rovouma."

" What is its size ? "

" It is about forty-five miles wide, and ten long."

" How shall we cross it ? "

" Cross it we cannot," said Mokoum. " There is but

one resource : we must go round either to the east or to the west."

At this intelligence the chiefs were much perplexed. In the forest they could not establish stations ; to pass round would involve them in an additional series of perhaps ten auxiliary triangles.

Here was a difficulty of no little magnitude. Encamping in the shade of a magnificent grove about half a mile from the forest, the astronomers assembled in council. The question of surveying across the mass of trees was at once set aside, and it now remained to determine whether they should make the circuit to the east or the west, since the meridian passed as nearly as possible through the centre of the forest. On this point arose a violent discussion between the Colonel and Strux. The two rivals recovered their old animosity, and the discussion ended in a serious altercation. Their colleagues attempted to interfere, but to no purpose. The Englishman wished to turn to the right, since that direction approached the route taken by Dr. Livingstone in his expedition to the Zambesi Falls, and the country would on that account be more known and frequented. The Russian, on the contrary, insisted on going to the left, but apparently for no other reason than to thwart the Colonel. The quarrel went so far that a separation between the members of the Commission seemed imminent. Zorn, Emery, Sir John, and Palander withdrew and left their chiefs to themselves. Such was their obstinacy that it seemed as if the survey must continue from this point in two oblique series of triangles.

The day passed away without any reconciliation, and the next morning Sir John, finding matters still in the same condition, proposed to Mokoum to beat the neighbourhood. Perhaps meanwhile the astronomers would come to an understanding: any way, some fresh venison would not be despised.

Mokoum, always ready, whistled to his dog Top, and the two hunters ventured several miles from the encampment. The conversation naturally turned on the subject of the difficulty.

"I expect," said the bushman, "we shall be encamped some time here. Our two chiefs are like ill-paired oxen, one pulls one way and the other another, and the consequence is that the waggon makes no headway."

"It is all very sad," answered Sir John, "and looks like a separation. The interests of science are compromised, otherwise I should be indifferent to it all. I should amuse myself with my gun until the rivals made it up."

"Do you think they *will* make it up? For my part, I am almost afraid that our halt will be indefinitely prolonged."

"I fear so, Mokoum," replied Sir John. "The matter is so trivial, and it is no question of science. Our chiefs would doubtless have yielded to a scientific argument, but they will never make concession in a pure matter of opinion. How unfortunate that the meridian happens to cross this forest!"

"Hang the forests!" exclaimed the bushman, "don't let them stop your measuring, if you want to measure. But I can't see the good of your getting at the length and breadth of the earth? Who will be any better off when every thing is reduced to feet and inches? I should just like to think of the globe as infinite; to measure it is to make it small. No, Sir John, if I were to live for ever, I could never understand the use of your operations."

Sir John could not help smiling. They had often debated the subject, and the ignorant child of nature could evidently not enter into the interest attached to the survey. Whenever Sir John attempted to convince him, he answered eloquently with arguments stamped with a genuine naturalness, of which Sir John, half-*savant* and half-hunter, could fully appreciate the charm.

Thus conversing, the hunters pursued the rock-hares, the shrill-toned plovers, the partridges (with brown, yellow, and black plumage), and other small game. But Sir John had all the sport to himself. The bushman seldom fired; he was pre-occupied. The quarrel between the two astronomers seemed to trouble him more than it did his companion, and the variety of game hardly attracted his notice.

In truth there was an idea floating through his brain, which, little by little, took more definite form. Sir John heard him talking to himself, and watched him as he quietly let the game pass by, as engrossed as Palander himself. Two or three times in the course of the day he drew near Sir John and said,—

"So you really think that Colonel Everest and Mr. Strux will not come to terms?"

Sir John invariably replied that agreement seemed unlikely, and that he feared there would be a separation between Englishmen and Russians. The last time Mokoum received this answer he added,—

"Well, you may be easy; I have found a means to satisfy both the chiefs. Before to-morrow, if the wind is favourable, they will have nothing to quarrel about."

"What do you mean to do, Mokoum?"

"Never mind, Sir John."

"Very well, I will leave it to you. You deserve to have your name preserved in the annals of science."

"That would be too great an honour for me, Sir John," answered the bushman, and then continued silently to ponder over his project. Sir John made no further inquiries, but could not at all guess how the bushman proposed to re-unite the two adversaries.

Towards evening the hunters returned to camp, and

found matters even worse than before. The oft-repeated intervention of Zorn and Emery had been of no avail, and the quarrel had now reached such a height that reconciliation seemed impossible. It appeared only too probable that the survey would be continued in two separate directions. The thought of this was sorrowful to Emery and Zorn, who were now so nearly bound by mutual sympathy. Sir John guessed their thoughts, and was eager to reassure them; but however much he was secretly disposed to trust to the bushman, he abstained from raising any hopes which might be fallacious.

Throughout the evening Mokoum did not leave his ordinary occupations. He arranged the sentinels, and took the usual precautions. Sir John began to think that he had forgotten his promise. Before going to rest he tried to sound Colonel Everest, whom he found immovably resolved that, unless Strux yielded, the English and Russians must part. "There are things," added the Colonel, in a tone of decision, "that cannot be borne, even from a colleague."

Sir John, very uneasy, retired to his bed, and being fatigued with his day's sport, was soon asleep. Towards eleven o'clock he was suddenly aroused by the natives running to and fro in the camp. He quickly rose, and found every one on their feet. The forest was on fire. In the dark night, against the black sky, the curtain of flame

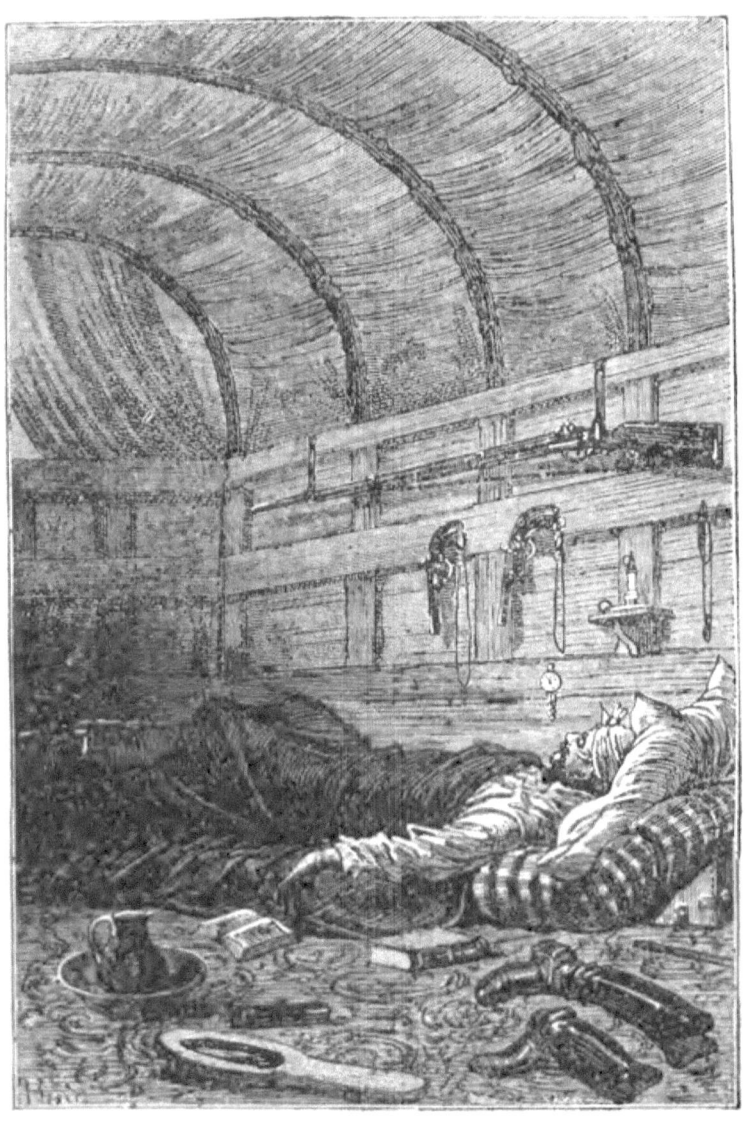

Sir John was soon asleep.—[Page 124.]

The Forest on Fire.—[Page 125.]

seemed to rise to the zenith; and in this incredibly short time the fire had extended for several miles.

Sir John looked at Mokoum, who, standing near, made no answer to his glance; but he at once understood. The fire was designed to open a road through that forest which had stood impervious for ages. The wind, from the south, was favourable. The air, rushing as from a ventilator, accelerated the conflagration, and furnished an ever fresh supply of oxygen. It animated the flames, and kept the kindled branches burning like a myriad brands. The scattered fragments became new centres for fresh outbreaks of flame; the scene of the fire became larger, and the heat grew intense. The dead wood piled under the dark foliage crackled, and ever and anon louder reports and a brighter light told that the resinous trees were burning like torches. Then followed explosions like cannonades, as the great trunks of ironwood burst asunder with a reverberation as of bombs. The sky reflected the glow, and the clouds carried the rosy glare high aloft. Showers of sparks emitted from the wreaths of smoke studded the heavens like red-hot stars.

Then, on every side, were heard the howls, shrieks, and bellowings of herds of bewildered hyenas, buffaloes, and lions; elephants rushed in every direction, like huge dark spectres, and disappeared beyond the horizon.

The fire continued throughout the following day and

night; and when day broke on the 14th a vast space, several miles wide, had been opened across the forest. A passage was now free for the meridian. The daring genius of Mokoum had arrested the disaster which threatened the survey.

CHAPTER XIV.

A DECLARATION OF WAR.

ALL pretext for quarrelling being now removed, the Colonel and Strux, somewhat rancorous at heart, recommenced their joint labours. About five miles to the left of the gap made by the conflagration, rose an eminence which would serve as the vertex of a new triangle. When the requisite observations were complete, the caravan set off across the burnt forest.

The road was paved with embers. The soil was still burning, and here and there smouldered stumps of trees, while a hot steam rose around. In many places lay the blackened carcases of animals which had been unable to make their escape. Wreaths of smoke gave evidence that the fire was not yet extinct, and might still be rekindled by the wind. Had the flames burst out again the caravan must inevitably have been destroyed. Towards the middle of the day, however, it was safely encamped at the foot of the hill. Here was a mass of rock which seemed to have been arranged by the hand of man. It was a kind of cromlech—a surprising erection to find in that locality—resembling the structures attributed to the Druids, and which ever furnish fresh interest to the archæologist. The most credible suggestion was that it must be the remains of some primitive African altar.

The two young astronomers and Sir John Murray wished to visit the fantastic construction, and, accompanied by the bushman, they ascended the slope. They were not above twenty paces from the cromlech when a man, hitherto concealed behind one of the massy stones at the base, appeared for a moment, and, descending the hill, stole quickly away into a thicket that had been untouched by the fire. The momentary glance was enough for the bushman. "A Makololo!" he cried, and rushed after the native. Sir John followed, and both in vain searched the wood. The native, knowing the short paths, had escaped where the most experienced hunter could not have traced him. When the incident was related to Colonel Everest he sent for Mokoum, and asked him who the man was? what he was doing? and why he had followed him?

"He is a Makololo, Colonel," replied Mokoum. "He belongs to one of the northern tribes that haunt the affluents of the Zambesi. Not only is he an enemy of us Bochjesmen, but he is a plunderer of all who venture into the country; he was spying us, and we shall be lucky if we have not cause to regret that we couldn't get hold of him."

"But what have we to fear from a band of robbers?" asked the Colonel; "are not our numbers sufficient to resist them?"

"At present, yes," replied the bushman; "but in the north these tribes are more frequent, and it is difficult to avoid them. If this Makololo is a spy, as I suspect, he will not fail in putting several hundred of these robbers on our track, and then, Colonel, I would not give a farthing for all your triangles."

The Colonel was vexed. He knew that the bushman was not the man to exaggerate danger, and that all he said ought to be duly weighed. The intentions of the native were certainly suspicious; his sudden appearance and immediate flight showed that he was caught deliberately spying. No doubt he would announce the approach of the Commission to the tribes of the north. There was, however, no help for it now; the caravan must continue its march with extra precautions.

On the 17th of August the astronomers completed their twenty-second triangle, and with it the third degree of the meridian. Finding by the map that the village of Kolobeng was about 100 miles to the north-east, they resolved to turn thither for a few days' rest. For nearly six months they had had no communication with the civilized world, and at Kolobeng, an important village and missionary station, they would probably hear news from Europe, besides being able to re-provision the caravan.

The remarkable cromlech was at once chosen as the landmark whence subsequent operations should commence, and the Colonel gave the signal for departure. With no further incident the caravan reached Kolobeng on the 22nd. The village was merely a mass of native huts, the uniformity of which was relieved by the depôt of the missionaries who had settled there. Formerly called Lepelolé, it is marked on some maps Litoubarouka. Here Dr. Livingstone stayed for some months in 1843, to learn the habits of the Bechuanas, or Bakouins, as they are more generally termed in this part of the country.

With all hospitality the missionaries received the Europeans, and put every available resource at their disposal. Livingstone's house was still to be seen, sacked and ruined, as when visited by Baldwin; the Boërs had not spared it in their incursion of 1852.

All eagerly asked for news from Europe; but their curiosity could not be immediately satisfied, as no courier had reached the mission in the last six months; but in about a week the principal said they expected journals and despatches, since they had already heard of the arrival of a carrier on the banks of the Upper Zambesi. A week was just the period that the astronomers desired for their rest, and all except Palander, who constantly revised his calculations, passed the time in a complete *far niente*. The stern Matthew Strux held himself aloof from his English colleagues, and Emery and Zorn took many walks in the neighbourhood. The firmest friendship united these two, and they believed that nothing could break the closeness of their sympathy.

On the 30th the eagerly-expected messenger arrived. He was a native of Kilmaine, a town by the delta of the Zambesi. A merchantman from the Mauritius, trading in gum and ivory, had landed on that coast early in July, and delivered the despatches for the missionaries. The papers were dated two months back, for the native had taken four weeks to ascend the Zambesi.

On the arrival of the messenger, the principal of the mission had handed to Colonel Everest a bundle of European newspapers, chiefly the *Times*, the *Daily News*, and the *Journal des Débats*. The intelligence they contained had, under the circumstances, a special importance, and produced an unexpected emotion among the entire party.

The members of the Commission were altogether in the chief room of the mission. Colonel Everest drew out the *Daily News* for the 13th of May, with the intention of reading aloud to his colleagues. Scarcely had he glanced at the first leading article, when his brow contracted, and the paper trembled in his hand. In a few moments he recovered his usual composure.

"What does the paper say, Colonel?" asked Sir John.

"It is grave news, gentlemen," said the Colonel, "that I have to communicate."

He kept the paper in his hand, and his colleagues waited eagerly for him to speak. To the surprise of all he rose, and, advancing to Matthew Strux, said,—

"Before communicating the intelligence conveyed in this paper, I should wish to make an observation to you."

"I am ready to hear any thing you may say," said Strux, much astonished.

The Colonel then said solemnly,—

"Mr. Strux, hitherto there has been between us a rivalry more personal than scientific, which has rendered our co-operation in the common cause somewhat difficult. This, I believe, is to be attributed to the fact of there being *two* of us at the head of this expedition. To avoid antagonism, there should be only one chief to every enterprise. You agree with me, do you not?"

Strux bowed in assent. The Colonel went on,—

"This position, unpleasant for each of us, must, through recent circumstances, now be changed. First, sir, let me say that I esteem you highly, as your position in the scientific world demands. I beg you to believe that I regret all that has passed between us."

"War is declared between England and Russia."—[Page 133.]

These words were uttered with great dignity, even with pride. There was no humiliation in the voluntary apology, so nobly expressed, and neither Strux nor his colleagues could guess his motive. Perhaps the Russian, not having the same incentive, was not equally disposed to forget any personal resentment. However, mastering his ill-feeling, he replied,—

"With you, Colonel, I think that no rivalry on our part should be permitted to injure the scientific work with which we are entrusted. I likewise hold *you* in the esteem that your talents deserve, and in future I will do all in my power to efface any personality from our relations. But you spoke of a change; I do not understand——"

"You will soon be made to understand, Mr. Strux," replied the Colonel, with a touch of sadness in his tone, "but first give me your hand."

"Here it is," rejoined Strux, with a slight hesitation. Without another word the astronomers joined hands.

"Now you are friends," cried Sir John.

"Alas! no," said the Colonel, dropping the Russian's hand; "henceforth we are enemies, separated by an abyss which must keep us apart even on the territory of science."

Then turning to his colleagues, he added,—

"Gentlemen, war is declared between England and Russia. See, the news is conveyed by these English, French, and Russian newspapers."

And, in truth, the war of 1854 had begun. The English, with their allies the French and Turks, were fighting before Sebastopol, and the Eastern question was being submitted to the ordeal of a naval conflict on the Black Sea.

The Colonel's words fell like a thunderbolt. The English and Russians, with their strong sentiment of nationality, started to their feet. Those three words, "War is declared," were enough. They were no longer companions united in a common labour, but already eyed one another as avowed antagonists. Such is the influence of these national duels on the heart of man. An instinctive impulse had divided the Europeans—Nicholas Palander himself yielding to the feeling: Emery and Zorn alone regarded each other with more of sadness than animosity, and regretted that they had not shaken hands before Colonel Everest's communication. No further conversation ensued; exchanging bows, English and Russians retired.

This novel situation, although it would not interrupt the survey, would render its continuation more difficult. For the interest of its country, each party desired to pursue the operations; but the measurements must be carried along two different meridians. In a formal interview subsequently arranged between the chiefs, it was decided by lot that the Russians should continue the meridian already begun, while the English should choose an arc 60 or 80 miles to the west, and unite it to the first by a series of

The Parting of Emery and Zorn.—[Page 135.]

auxiliary triangles; they would then continue their survey as far as lat. 20°.

All these arrangements were made without any outbreak: personal rivalry was swallowed up by national feeling, and the Colonel and Strux did not exchange an uncivil word, but kept within the strictest limits of politeness.

The caravan was equally divided, each party preserving its own stores. The steam-boat fell by lot to the Russians.

Mokoum, especially attached to Sir John, followed the English caravan. The pioneer, equally experienced, headed the Russians. Each party retained its instruments and one of the registers.

On the 31st of August the Commission divided. The English cordially thanked the missionaries for their kind hospitality, and started first to connect their last station with their new meridian.

If, before their departure, any one had entered the privacy of the inner room, he would have seen Emery grasping the hand of Zorn, once his friend, but now, by the will of their Majesties the Queen of England and the Czar of Russia, no longer friend, but foe.

CHAPTER XV.

A GEOMETRIC PROGRESSION.

AFTER the separation the English astronomers continued their labours with the same care and precision as hitherto. Three had now to do the work of six, and consequently the survey advanced more slowly, and was attended with more fatigue; but they were not the men to spare themselves; the desire that the Russians should not surpass them in any way sustained them in their task, to which they gave all their time and thoughts. Emery had to indulge in fewer reveries, and Sir John could not so often spare his time for hunting. A new programme was drawn up, assigning to each astronomer his proper share of the labour. Sir John and the Colonel undertook all observations both in the sky and in the field; while Emery replaced Palander as calculator. All questions were decided in common, and there was no longer any fear that disagreement should arise. Mokoum was still the guide and hunter to the caravan. The English sailors, who formed half the crew of the "Queen and Czar," had, of course, followed their countrymen; and although the Russians were in possession of the steam-vessel, the India-rubber boat, which was large enough for ordinary purposes, was the property of the English. The provision-waggons were divided, thus impartially ensuring the revictualling of each caravan. The natives likewise had to be severed into two equal troops, not without some natural signs of displeasure on their part; far from their own pasturages and water-courses, in a region inhabited by wandering tribes hostile to the tribes of the south, they could scarcely be reconciled to the prospect of separation. But at length, by the help of the bushman and the pioneer, who told them that the two detachments would be comparatively a short distance apart, they consented to the arrangement.

On leaving Kolobeng the English caravan re-entered the burnt forest and arrived at the cromlech which had served for their last station. Operations were resumed, and a large triangle carried the observers at once ten or twelve miles to the west of the old meridian.

Six days later the auxiliary series of triangles was finished, and Colonel Everest and his colleagues, after consulting the maps, chose the new arc one degree west of the other, being 23° east of the meridian of Greenwich. They were not more than sixty miles from the Russians, but this distance put any collision between the two parties out of the question, as it was improbable that their triangles would cross.

All through September the weather was fine and clear. The country was fertile and varied, but scantily populated. The forests, which were few, being broken by wide, open tracts, and with occasional mounds occurring in the prairies, made the district extremely favourable for the observations. The region was well provided with natural productions. The sweet scent of many of the flowers attracted swarms of scarabæi, and more especially a kind of bee as nearly as possible like the European, depositing in clefts of rocks and holes of trees a white liquid honey with a delicious flavour. Occasionally at night large animals ventured near the camp; there were giraffes, varieties of antelopes, hyenas, rhinoceroses, and elephants. But Sir John would not be distracted, he resolutely discarded his rifle for his telescope.

Under these circumstances, Mokoum and some of the natives became purveyors to the caravan, and Sir John had some difficulty in restraining his excitement when he heard the report of their guns. The bushman shot three prairie-bufialoes, the Bokolokolos of the Bechuanas, formidable animals, with glossy black skins, short strong legs, fierce eyes, and small heads crowned with thick black horns. They were a welcome addition to the fresh venison which formed the ordinary fare.

The natives prepared the buffalo-meat as the Indians of the north do their pemmican. The Europeans watched their proceedings with interest, though at first with some repugnance. The flesh, after being cut into thin slices and dried in the sun, was wrapped in a tanned skin, and beaten with flails till it was reduced to a powder. It was then pressed tightly into leathern sacks, and moistened with boiling tallowy suet collected from the animal itself. To this they added some marrow and berries, whose saccharine matter modified the nitrous elements of the meat. This compound, after being mixed and beaten, formed, when cold, a cake as hard as a stone. Mokoum, who considered his pemmican a national delicacy, begged the astronomers to taste the preparation. At first they found it extremely unpalatable, but, becoming accustomed to the flavour, they soon learnt to partake of it with great relish. Highly nourishing, and not at all likely to be tainted, containing, moreover, its nutritive elements closely compacted, this pemmican was exactly suited to meet the wants of a caravan travelling in an unknown country. The bushman soon had several hundred pounds in reserve, and they were thus secure from any immediate want.

Days and nights passed away in observations. Emery was always thinking of his friend, and deploring the fate which had so suddenly severed the bond of their friendship. He had no one to sympathize with his admiration of the wild characteristics of the scenery, and, with something of Palander's enthusiasm, found refuge in his calculations. Colonel Everest was cold and calm as ever, exhibiting no interest in any thing beyond his professional pursuits. As for Sir John, he suppressed his murmurs, but sighed over the loss of his freedom. Fortune, however, sometimes made amends; for although he had no leisure for hunting, the wild beasts occasionally took the initiative, and came near, interrupting his observations. He then considered defence legitimate, and rejoiced to be able to make the duties of the astronomer and of the hunter to be compatible.

One day he had a serious rencontre with an old rhinoceros, which cost him "rather dear." For some time the animal had been prowling about the flanks of the caravan. By the blackness of his skin Mokoum had recognized the "chucuroo" (such is the native for this animal) as a dangerous beast, and one which, more agile than the white species, often attacks man and beast without any provocation.

On this day Sir John and Mokoum had set off to reconnoitre a hill six miles away, on which the Colonel wished to establish an indicating-post. With a certain foreboding, Sir John had brought his rifle with conical shot instead of his ordinary gun; for although the rhinoceros had not been seen for two days, yet he did not consider it

"The Rhinoceros!" exclaimed Sir John.—[Page 141.]

advisable to traverse unarmed an unknown country. Mokoum and his companions had already unsuccessfully chased the beast, which probably now had abandoned its designs. There was no reason to regret the precaution. The adventurers had reached the summit of the hill, when at the base, close to a thicket, of no large extent, appeared the chucuroo. He was a formidable animal; his small eyes sparkled, and his horns, planted firmly one over the other on his bony nose, furnished a most powerful weapon of attack.

The bushman caught sight of him first, as he crouched about half a mile distant in a grove of lentisk.

"Sir John," he cried, "fortune favours you : here is your chucuroo!"

"The rhinoceros!" exclaimed Sir John, with kindling eyes, for he had never before been so near the animal.

"Yes; a magnificent beast, and he seems inclined to cut off our retreat," said the bushman. "Why he should attack us, I can hardly say; his tribe is not carnivorous : but any way, there he is, and we must hunt him out."

"Is it possible for him to get up here to us?" asked Sir John.

"No; his legs are too short and thick, but he will wait."

"Well, let him wait," said Sir John; "and when we have examined this station, we will try and get him out."

They then proceeded with their reconnoitring, and chose

a spot on which to erect the indicating-post. They also noticed other eminences to the north-west which would be of use in constructing a subsequent triangle.

Their work ended, Sir John turned to the bushman, saying, "When you like, Mokoum."

"I am at your orders, Sir John: the rhinoceros is still waiting."

"Well, let us go down, a ball from my rifle will soon settle matters."

"A ball!" cried Mokoum; "you don't know a rhinoceros. He won't fall with one ball, however well it may be aimed."

"Nonsense!" began Sir John, "that is because people don't use conical shot."

"Conical or round," rejoined the bushman, "the first will not bring down such an animal as that."

"Well," said Sir John, carried away by his self-confidence, "as you have your doubts, I will show you what our European weapons can do."

And he loaded his rifle, to be ready to take aim as soon as he should be at a convenient distance.

"One moment, Sir John," said the bushman, rather piqued, "will you bet with me?"

"Certainly," said Sir John.

"I am only a poor man," continued Mokoum, "but I will willingly bet you half-a-crown against your first ball."

"Done!" replied Sir John instantly. "Half-a-crown to you if the rhinoceros doesn't fall to my first shot."

The hunters descended the steep slope, and were soon posted within range of the rhinoceros. The beast was perfectly motionless, and on that account presented an easy aim.

Sir John thought his chance so good, that at the last moment he turned to Mokoum and said,—

"Do you keep to your bargain?"

"Yes," replied the bushman.

The rhinoceros still being as motionless as a target, Sir John could aim wherever he thought the blow would be mortal. He chose the muzzle, and, his pride being roused, he aimed with the utmost care, and fired. The ball failed in reaching the flesh; it had merely shattered to fragments the extremity of one of the horns. The animal did not appear to experience the slightest shock.

"That counts nothing," said the bushman, "you didn't touch the flesh."

"Yes, it counts," replied Sir John, rather vexed; "I have lost my wager. But come now, double or quits?"

"As you please, Sir John, but you will lose."

"We shall see."

The rifle was carefully re-loaded, and Sir John, taking rather a random aim, fired a second time; but meeting the horny skin of the haunch, the ball, notwithstanding its force, fell to the ground. The rhinoceros moved a few steps.

"A crown to me," said Mokoum.

"Will you stake it again?" asked Sir John, "double or quits."

"By all means," said Mokoum.

This time Sir John, who had begun to get angry, regained his composure, and aimed at the animal's forehead. The ball rebounded, as if it had struck a metal plate.

"Half-a-sovereign," said the bushman calmly.

"Yes, and another," cried Sir John, exasperated.

The shot penetrated the skin, and the rhinoceros made a tremendous bound; but instead of falling, he rushed furiously upon the bushes, which he tore and crushed violently.

"I think he still moves," said the bushman quietly.

Sir John was beside himself; his composure again deserted him, and he risked the sovereign he owed the bushman on a fifth ball. He continued to lose again and again, but persisted in doubling the stake at every shot. At length the animal, pierced to the heart, fell, impotent to rise to its feet.

Sir John uttered a loud hurrah; he had killed his rhinoceros. He had forgotten his disappointment, but he did not forget his bets. It was startling to find that the perpetually redoubled stakes had mounted at the ninth shot to 32*l*. Sir John congratulated himself on his escape from such a debt of honour; but in his enthusiasm he presented Mokoum with several gold pieces which the bushman received with his usual equanimity.

CHAPTER XVI.

DANGER IN DISGUISE.

By the end of September the astronomers had accomplished half their task. Their diminished numbers added to their fatigue, so that, notwithstanding their zeal, they occasionally had to recruit themselves by resting for several days. The heat was very overpowering. October in lat. 24° S. corresponds to April in Algeria, and for some hours after mid-day work was impossible. The bushman was alone uneasy at the delay, for he was aware that the arc was about to pass through a singular region called a "karroo," similar to that at the foot of the Roggeveld mountains in Cape Colony. In the damp season this district presents signs of the greatest fertility; after a few days of rain the soil is covered with a dense verdure; in a very short time flowers and plants spring up every where; pasturage increases, and water-courses are formed; troops of antelopes descend from the heights and take possession of these unexpected prairies. But this strange effort of nature is of short duration. In a month, or six weeks at most, all the moisture is absorbed by the sun; the soil becomes hardened, and chokes the fresh germs; vegetation disappears in a few days; the animals fly the region; and where for a while there was a rich fertility, the desert again asserts its dominion.

This karroo had to be crossed before reaching the permanent desert bordering on Lake Ngami. The bushman was naturally eager to traverse this region before the extreme aridity should have exhausted the springs. He explained his reasons to the Colonel, who perfectly understood, and promised to hurry on the work, without suffering its precision to be affected. Since, on account of the state of the atmosphere, measuring was not always practicable, the operations were not unfrequently retarded, and the bushman became seriously concerned lest when they reached the karroo its character of fertility should have disappeared.

Meanwhile the astronomers could not fail to appreciate the magnificence around. Never had they been in finer country. In spite of the high temperature, the streams kept up a constant freshness, and thousands of flocks would have found inexhaustible pasturage. Clumps of luxuriant trees rose here and there, giving the prospect at times the appearance of an English park.

Colonel Everest was comparatively indifferent to these beauties, but the others were fully alive to the romantic aspect of this temporary relief to the African deserts. Emery now especially regretted the alienation of his friend Zorn, and often thought how they would have mutually delighted in the charming scenery around them.

The advance of the caravan was enlivened by the movements as well as by the song-notes of a variety of birds. Some of these were edible, and the hunters shot some brace of "korans," a sort of bustard peculiar to the South African plains, and some "dikkops," whose flesh is very delicate eating. They were frequently followed by voracious crows, instinctively seeking to avert attention from their eggs in their nests of sand. In addition to these, blue cranes with white throats, red flamingoes, like flames in the thinly scattered brushwood, herons, curlews, snipes, "kalas," often perching on a buffalo's neck, plovers, ibises, which might have flown from some hieroglyphic obelisk, hundreds of enormous pelicans marching in file,—all were observed to find congenial habitats in this district, where man alone is the stranger. But of all the varieties of the feathered race, the most noticeable was the ingenious weaver-bird, whose green nests, woven with rushes and blades of grass, hung like immense pears from the branches of the willows. Emery, taking them for a new species of fruit, gathered one or two, and was much surprised to hear them twitter like sparrows. There seemed some excuse for the ancient travellers in Africa, who reported that

The Advance of the Caravan. — (Page 148.)

certain trees in the country bore fruit producing living birds.

The karroo was reached while still it was lovely in its verdure. Gnus, with their pointed hoofs, caamas, elks, chamois, and gazelles abounded. Sir John could not resist the temptation to obtain two days' leave from the Colonel, which he devoted with all his energy to his favourite pastime. Under the guidance of the bushman, while Emery accompanied as an amateur, he obtained many a success to inscribe in his journal, and many a trophy to carry back to his Highland home. His hand, skilful with the delicate instruments of the survey, was at home still more on his gun ; and his eye, keen to discern the remotest of stars, was quick to detect the merest movement of a gazelle. It was ever with something of self-denial that he laid aside the character of the hunter to resume the duties of the astronomer. The bushman's uneasiness was ere long renewed. On the second day of Sir John's interval of recreation, Mokoum had espied, nearly two miles to the right, a herd of about twenty of the species of antelope known as the oryx. He told Sir John at once, and advised him to take advantage of the fortune that awaited him, adding that the oryx was extremely difficult to capture, and could outstrip the fleetest horse, and that Cumming himself had not brought down more than four.

This was more than enough to arouse the Englishman.

He chose his best gun, his best horse, and his best dogs, and, in his impatience preceding the bushman, he turned towards the copse bordering the plain where the antelopes had been seen. In an hour they reined in their horses, and Mokoum, concealed by a grove of sycamores, pointed out to his companion the herd grazing several hundred paces to leeward. He remarked that one oryx kept apart.

"He is a sentinel," he said, "and doubtless cunning enough. At the slightest danger, he will give his signal, and the whole troop will make their escape. We must fire from a long distance, and hit at the first shot."

Sir John nodded in reply, and sought for a favourable position.

The oryxes continued quietly grazing. The sentinel, as though the breeze had brought suspicions of danger, often raised his head, and looked warily around. But he was too far away for the hunters to fire at him with success, and to chase the herd over the plain was out of the question. The only hope of a lucky issue was that the herd might approach the copse.

Fortune seemed propitious. Gradually following the lead of the sentinel male, the herd drew near the wood, their instinct, perchance, making them aware that it was safer than the plain. When their direction was seen, the bushman asked his companion to dismount. The horses were tied

The Hunters glided through the Creepers and Brushwood.—[Page 151.]

to a sycamore, and their heads covered to secure them from taking alarm.

Followed by the dogs, the hunters glided through the creepers and brushwood till they were within three hundred paces of the troop. Then, crouching in ambush, and waiting with loaded guns, they could admire the beauty of the animals. By a strange freak of nature, the females were armed with horns more formidable than those of the males. The whole herd approached the wood, and awhile remained stationary. The sentinel oryx, as it seemed, was urging them to leave the plain; he appeared to be driving them, something like a sheep-collie congregates a flock, into a compact mass. The herd seemed strangely indifferent, and indisposed to submit to the guidance of their leader. The bushman was perplexed; he could not understand the relative movements of the sentinel and the herd.

Sir John began to get impatient. He fidgeted with his rifle, sometimes wanting to fire, sometimes to advance; and the bushman had some trouble to restrain him. An hour passed away in this manner, when suddenly one of the dogs gave a loud bark, and rushed towards the plain. The bushman felt angry enough to send a ball into the excited brute. The oryxes fled, and Sir John saw at once that pursuit was useless; in a few seconds they were no more than black specks in the grass. But to the bushman's astonishment it was not the old male which had given the signal for flight.

The oryx remained in its place, without attempting to follow, and only tried to hide in the grass.

"Strange," said the bushman; "what ails the creature? Is he hurt, or crippled with age?"

"We shall soon see," said Sir John, advancing towards the animal.

The oryx crouched more and more in the grass; only the tips of his long horns were visible above the surface; but as he did not try to escape, Sir John could easily get near him. When within a hundred paces he took aim, and fired. The ball had struck the head, for the horns sunk into the grass. The hunters ran hastily to the spot. The bushman held in his hand his hunting-knife, in case the animal should still live. This precaution was unnecessary; the oryx was so dead, that when Sir John took hold of the horns, he pulled nothing but an empty flabby skin, containing not so much as a bone.

"By St. Andrew! these things happen to no one but me," he cried, in a tone so comical that any one but the immovable Mokoum would have laughed outright. But Mokoum did not even smile. His compressed lips and contracted brow showed him to be utterly bewildered. With his arms crossed, he looked quickly right and left.

Suddenly he caught sight of a little red leather bag, ornamented with arabesques, on the ground, which he picked up and examined carefully.

The empty Oryx Skin.—[Page 152.]

"What's that?" asked Sir John.

"A Makololo's pouch," replied Mokoum.

"How did it get there?"

"The owner let it fall as he fled."

"What do you mean?"

"I mean," said Mokoum, clenching his fists, "that the Makololo was in the oryx skin, and you have missed him."

Sir John had not time to express his astonishment, when Mokoum, observing a movement in the distance, with all speed seized his gun and fired.

He and Sir John hastened to the suspected spot. But the place was empty : they could perceive by the trampled grass that some one had just been there ; but the Makololo was gone, and it was useless to think of pursuit across the prairie.

The two hunters returned, much discomposed. The presence of a Makololo at the cromlech, together with his disguise, not unfrequently adopted by oryx hunters, showed that he had systematically followed the caravan. It was not without design that he was keeping watch upon the Europeans and their escort. The more they advanced to the north, the greater danger there would be of being attacked by the plunderers.

Emery was inclined to banter Sir John on his return from his holiday without booty ; but Sir John replied,—

"I hadn't a chance, William ; the first oryx I hunted was dead before I shot at him."

CHAPTER XVII.

AN UNEXPECTED BLIGHT.

AFTER the oryx hunt the bushman had a long conversation with the Colonel. He felt sure, he said, that they were watched and followed, and that the only reason why they had not been attacked before was because the Makololos wished to get them farther north, where their hordes were larger. The question thus arose whether, in presence of this danger, they should retrace their steps; but they were reluctant to suffer that which nature had favoured to be interrupted by the attacks of a few African savages. The Colonel, aware of the importance of the question, asked the bushman to tell him all he knew about the Makololos.

Mokoum explained that they were the most northerly branch of the great tribe of the Bechuanas. In 1850 Dr. Livingstone, during his first journey to the Zambesi, was received at Seshcki, the usual residence of Sebitouani, the chief of the Makololos. This native was a man of remarkable intelligence, and a formidable warrior. In 1824 he had menaced the Cape frontier, and, little by little, had gained an ascendency over the tribes of Central Africa, and had united them in a compact group. In the year before the arrival of the Anglo-Russian expedition the chief had died in Livingstone's arms, and his son Sekeleton succeeded him.

At first Sekeleton was very friendly towards the Europeans who visited the Zambesi, and Dr. Livingstone had no complaint to make. But after the departure of the famous traveller, not only strangers but the neighbouring tribes were harassed by Sekeleton and his warriors. To these vexations succeeded pillage on a large scale, and the Makololos scoured the district between Lake Ngami and the Upper Zambesi. Consequently nothing was more dangerous than for a caravan to venture across this region without a considerable escort, especially when its progress had been previously known.

Such was the history given by Mokoum. He said that he thought it right to tell the Colonel the whole truth, adding, that for his own part (if the Colonel so wished) he should not hesitate to continue the march.

Colonel Everest consulted with his colleagues, and it was settled that the work, at all risks, should be continued. Something more than half of the project was now accomplished, and, whatever happened, the English owed it to themselves and their country not to abandon their undertaking. The series of triangles was resumed. On the 27th the tropic of Capricorn was passed, and on the 3rd of November, with the completion of the forty-first triangle, a fifth degree was added to the meridian.

For a month the survey went on rapidly, without meeting a single natural obstacle. Mokoum, always on the alert, kept a constant look-out at the head and flanks of the caravan, and forbade the hunters to venture too great a distance away. No immediate danger, however, seemed to threaten the little troop, and they were sanguine that the bushman's fears might prove groundless. There was no further trace of the native who, after eluding them at the cromlech, had taken so strange a part in the oryx chase: nor did any other aggressor appear. Still, at various intervals, the bushman observed signs of trepidation among the Bochjesmen under his command. The incidents of the flight from the old cromlech, and the stratagem of the oryx hunt, could not be concealed from them, and they were perpetually expecting an attack. A deadly antipathy existed between tribe and tribe, and, in the event of a collision, the defeated party could entertain no hope of mercy. The Bochjesmen were already 300 miles from their home, and there was every prospect of their being carried 200 more. It is true that, before engaging them, Mokoum had been careful to inform them of the length and difficulties of the journey, and they were not men to shrink from fatigue; but now, when to these was added the danger of a conflict with implacable enemies, regret was mingled with murmuring, and dissatisfaction was exhibited with ill-humour, and although Mokoum pretended neither to hear nor to see, he was silently conscious of an increasing anxiety.

On the 2nd of December a circumstance occurred which still further increased the spirit of complaint amongst this superstitious people, and provoked them to a kind of rebellion. Since the previous evening the weather had become dull. The atmosphere, saturated with vapour, gave signs of being heavily charged with electric fluid. There was every prospect of the recurrence of one of the storms which in this tropical district are seldom otherwise than violent. During the morning the sky became covered with sinister-looking clouds, piled together like bales of down of contrasted colours, the yellowish hue distinctly relieving the masses of dark grey. The sun was wan, the heat was overpowering, and the barometer fell rapidly; the air was so still that not a leaf fluttered.

Although the astronomers had not been unconscious of the change of weather, they had not thought it necessary to suspend their labours. Emery, attended by two sailors and four natives in charge of a waggon, was sent two miles east of the meridian to establish a post for the vertex of the next triangle. He was occupied in securing his point of sight, when a current of cold air caused a rapid condensation, which appeared to contribute immediately to a development of electric matter. Instantly there fell a violent shower of hail, and by a rare phenomenon the hailstones were luminous, so that it seemed to be raining drops of boiling silver. The storm increased; sparks flashed from the ground, and jets of light gleamed from the iron settings of the waggon. Dr. Livingstone relates that he has seen tiles broken, and horses and antelopes killed, by the violence of these hail-storms.

Without losing a moment, Emery left his work for the purpose of calling his men to the waggon, which would afford better shelter than a tree. But he had hardly left the top of the hill, when a dazzling flash, instantly followed by a peal of thunder, inflamed the air.

Emery was thrown down, and lay prostrate, as though he were actually dead. The two sailors, dazzled for a moment, were not long in rushing towards him, and were relieved to find that the thunderbolt had spared him. He had been enveloped by the fluid, which, collected by the compass which he held in his hand, had been diverted in its course, so as to leave him not seriously injured. Raised by the sailors, he soon came to himself; but he had narrowly escaped. Two natives, twenty paces apart, lay lifeless at the foot of the post. One had been struck by the full force of the thunderbolt, and was a black and shattered corpse, while his clothes remained entire; the other had

Emery and two Natives struck by Lightning.—[Page 158.]

been locally struck on the skull by the destructive fluid, and had been killed at once. The three men had been undeniably struck by a single flash. This trisection of a flash of lightning is an unusual but not unknown occurrence, and the angular division was very large. The Bochjesmen were at first overwhelmed by the sudden death of their comrades, but soon, in spite of the cries of the sailors and at the risk of being struck themselves, they rushed back to the camp. The two sailors, having first provided for the protection of Emery, conveyed the two dead bodies to the waggon, and then found shelter for themselves, being sorely bruised by the hailstones, which fell like a shower of marbles. For three quarters of an hour the storm continued to rage; the hail then abated so as to allow the waggon to return to camp.

The news of the death of the natives had preceded them, and had produced a deplorable effect on the minds of the Bochjesmen, who already looked upon the trigonometrical operations with the terror of superstition. They assembled in secret council, and some more timid than the rest declared they would go no farther. The rebellious disposition began to look serious, and it took all the bushman's influence to arrest an actual revolt. Colonel Everest offered the poor men an increase of pay; but contentment was not to be restored without much trouble. It was a matter of emergency; had the natives deserted, the position of the caravan, without escort and without drivers, would have been perilous in the extreme. At length, however, the difficulty was overcome, and after the burial of the natives, the camp was raised, and the little troop proceeded to the hill where the two had met their death.

Emery felt the shock for some days: his left hand, which had held the compass, was almost paralyzed; but after a time it recovered, and he was able to resume his work.

For eighteen days no special incident occurred. The Makololos did not appear, and Mokoum, though still distrustful, exhibited fewer indications of alarm. They were not more than fifty miles from the desert; and the karroo was still verdant, and enriched by abundant water. They thought that neither man nor beast could want for any thing in this region so rich in game and pasturage; but they had reckoned without the locusts, against whose appearance there is no security in the agricultural districts of South Africa.

On the evening of the 20th, about an hour before sunset the camp was arranged for the night. A light northerly breeze refreshed the atmosphere. The three Englishmen and Mokoum, resting at the foot of a tree, discussed their plans for the future. It was arranged that during the night the astronomers should take the altitude of some stars, in order accurately to find their latitude. Every thing seemed favourable for the operations; in a cloudless sky the moon

A strange Cloud.—[Page 161.]

was nearly new, and the constellations might be expected to be clear and resplendent. Great was the disappointment, therefore, when Emery, rising and pointing to the north, said,—

"The horizon is overcast: I begin to fear our anticipations of a fine night will hardly be verified."

"Yes," replied Sir John, "I see a cloud is rising, and if the wind should freshen, it might overspread the sky."

"There is not another storm coming, I hope," interposed the Colonel.

"We are in the tropics," said Emery, "and it would not be surprising; for to-night I begin to have misgivings about our observations."

"What is your opinion, Mokoum?" asked the Colonel of the bushman.

Mokoum looked attentively towards the north. The cloud was bounded by a long clear curve, as definite as though traced by a pair of compasses. It marked off a section of some miles on the horizon, and its appearance, black as smoke, seemed to excite the apprehensions of the bushman. At times it reflected a reddish light from the setting sun, as though it were rather a solid mass than any collection of vapour. Without direct reply to the Colonel's appeal, Mokoum simply said that it was strange.

In a few minutes one of the Bochjesmen announced that

M

the horses and cattle showed signs of agitation, and would not be driven to the interior of the camp.

"Well, let them stay outside," said Mokoum; and in answer to the suggestion that there would be danger from the wild beasts around, he added significantly, "Oh, the wild beasts will be too much occupied to pay any attention to them."

After the native had gone back, Colonel Everest turned to ask what the bushman meant; but he had moved away, and was absorbed in watching the advance of the cloud, of which, too accurately, he was aware of the origin.

The dark mass approached. It hung low and appeared to be but a few hundred feet from the ground. Mingling with the sound of the wind was heard a peculiar rustling, which seemed to proceed from the cloud itself. At this moment, above the cloud against the sky, appeared thousands of black specks, fluttering up and down, plunging in and out, and breaking the distinctness of the outline.

"What are those moving specks of black?" asked Sir John.

"They are vultures, eagles, falcons, and kites," answered Mokoum, "from afar they have followed the cloud, and will never leave it until it is destroyed or dispersed."

"But the cloud?"

"Is not a cloud at all," answered the bushman, extending his hand towards the sombre mass, which by this time had spread over a quarter of the sky. "It is a living host; to say the truth, it is a swarm of locusts."

The hunter was not mistaken. The Europeans were about to witness one of those terrible invasions of grasshoppers which are unhappily too frequent, and in one night change the most fertile country into an arid desert. These locusts, now arriving by millions, were the "grylli devastorii" of the naturalists, and travellers have seen for a distance of fifty miles the beach covered with piles of these insects to the height of four feet.

"Yes," continued the bushman, "these living clouds are a true scourge to the country, and it will be lucky if we escape without harm."

"But we have no crops and pasturages of our own," said the Colonel; "what have we to fear?"

"Nothing, if they merely pass over our heads; every thing, if they settle on the country over which we must travel. They will not leave a leaf on the trees, nor a blade of grass on the ground; and you forget, Colonel, that if our own sustenance is secure, that of our animals is not. What do you suppose will become of us in the middle of a devastated district?"

The astronomers were silent for a time, and contemplated the animated mass before them. The cries of the eagles and falcons, who were devouring the insects by thousands, sounded above the redoubled murmur.

"Do you think they will settle here?" said Emery.

"I fear so," answered Mokoum, "the wind carries them here direct. The sun is setting, and the fresh evening breeze will bear them down; should they settle on the trees, bushes, and prairies, why, then I tell you——;" but the bushman could not finish his sentence. In an instant the enormous cloud which overshadowed them settled on the ground. Nothing could be seen as far as the horizon but the thickening mass. The camp was bestrewed; waggons and tents alike were veiled beneath the living hail. The Englishmen, moving knee-deep in the insects, crushed them by hundreds at every step.

Although there was no lack of agencies at work for their destruction, their aggregate defied all check. The birds, with hoarse cries, darted down from above, and devoured them greedily; from below, the snakes consumed them in enormous quantities; the horses, buffaloes, mules, and dogs fed on them with great relish; and lions and hyenas, elephants and rhinoceroses, swallowed them down by bushels. The very Bochjesmen welcomed these "shrimps of the air" like celestial manna; the insects even preyed on each other, but their numbers still resisted all sources of destruction.

The bushman entreated the English to taste the dainty. Thousands of young locusts, of a green colour, an inch to an inch and a half long, and about as thick as a quill, were caught. Before they have deposited their eggs, they are considered a great delicacy by connoisseurs, and are more tender than the old insects, which are of a yellowish tinge, and sometimes measure four inches in length. After half an hour's boiling and seasoning with salt, pepper, and vinegar, the bushman served up a tempting dish to the three Englishmen. The insects, dismembered of head, legs, and skin, were eaten just like shrimps, and were found extremely savoury. Sir John, who ate some hundreds, recommended his people to take advantage of the opportunity to make a large provision.

At night they were all about to seek their usual beds; but the interior of the waggons had not escaped the invasion. It was impossible to enter without crushing the locusts, and to sleep under such conditions was not an agreeable prospect. Accordingly, as the night was clear and the stars bright, the astronomers were rejoiced to pursue their contemplated operations, and deemed it more pleasant than burying themselves to the neck in a coverlet of locusts. Moreover, they would not have had a moment's sleep, on account of the howling of the beasts which were attracted by their unusual prey.

The next day the sun rose in a clear horizon, and commenced its course over a brilliant sky foreboding heat. A dull rustling of scales among the locusts showed that they were about to carry their devastations elsewhere; and towards eight o'clock the mass rose like the unfurling of an immense veil, and obscured the sun. It grew dusk as if night were returning, and with the freshening of the wind the whole mass was in motion. For two hours, with a deafening noise, the cloud passed over the darkened camp, and disappeared beyond the western horizon.

After their departure the bushman's predictions were found to be entirely realized. All was demolished, and the soil was brown and bare. Every branch was stripped to utter nakedness. It was like a sudden winter settling in the height of summer, or like the dropping of a desert into the midst of a land of plenty. The Oriental proverb which describes the devastating fury of the Osmanlis might justly be applied to these locusts, "Where the Turk has passed, the grass springs up no more."

CHAPTER XVIII.

THE DESERT.

IT was indeed no better than a desert which now lay before the travellers. When, on the 25th of December, they completed the measurement of another degree, and reached the northern boundary of the karroo, they found no difference between the district they had been traversing and the new country, the real desert, arid and scorching, over which they were now about to pass. The animals belonging to the caravan suffered greatly from the dearth alike of pasturage and water. The last drops of rain in the pools had dried up, and it was an acrid soil, a mixture of clay and sand, very unfavourable to vegetation. The waters of the rainy season filtered quickly through the sandy strata, so that the region was incapable of preserving for any length of time a particle of moisture. More than once has Dr. Livingstone carried his adventurous explorations across one of these barren districts. The very atmosphere was so dry, that iron left in the open air did not rust, and the distinguished traveller relates that the leaves hung weak and shrivelled; that the mimosas remained closed by day as well as by night; that the scarabæi, laid on the ground, expired in a few seconds; and that the mercury in the ball of a thermometer buried three inches in the soil rose at midday to 134° Fahrenheit.

These records which Livingstone had made were now verified by the astronomers between the karroo and Lake Ngami. The suffering and fatigue, especially of the animals, continually increased, and the dry dusty grass afforded them but little nourishment. Nothing ventured on the desert; the birds had flown beyond the Zambesi for fruit and flowers, and the wild beasts shunned the plain which offered them no prey. During the first fortnight in January the hunters caught sight of a few couples of those antelopes which are able to exist without water for several weeks. There were some oryxes like those in whose pursuit Sir John had sustained so great a disappointment, and there were besides, some dappled, soft-eyed caamas, which venture beyond the green pasturages, and which are much esteemed for the quality of their flesh.

To travel under that burning sun through the stifling atmosphere, to work for days and nights in the oppressive sultriness, was fatiguing in the extreme. The reserve of water evaporated continuously, so they were obliged to ration themselves to a painfully limited allowance. How-

Crossing the Desert.—[Page 169.]

ever, such were their zeal and courage that they mastered all their troubles, and not a single detail of their task was neglected. On the 25th of January they completed their seventh degree, the number of triangles constructed having amounted to fifty-seven.

Only a comparatively small portion of the desert had now to be traversed, and the bushman thought that they would be able to reach Lake Ngami before their provision was exhausted. The Colonel and his companions thus had definite hopes, and were inspirited to persevere. But the hired Bochjesmen, who knew nothing of any scientific ardour, and who had been long ago reluctant to pursue their journey, could hardly be encouraged to hold out: unquestionably they suffered greatly, and were objects for commiseration. Already, too, some beasts of burden, overcome by hard work and scanty food, had been left behind, and it was to be feared that more would fall into the same helpless condition. Mokoum had a difficult task to perform, and as murmurs and recriminations increased, his influence more and more lost its weight. It became evident that the want of water would be a serious obstacle, and that the expedition must either retrace its steps, or, at the risk of meeting the Russians, turn to the right of the meridian, to seek some of the villages which were known to be scattered along Livingstone's route.

It was not long, however, before the bushman one morning came to the Colonel, and declared himself powerless against the increasing difficulties. The drivers, he said, refused to obey him; and there were continued scenes of insubordination, in which all the natives joined. The Colonel perfectly well understood the situation; but stern to himself, he was stern to others. He refused to suspend his operations, and declared that although he went alone, he would continue to advance. His two companions of course agreed, and professed themselves ready to follow him. Renewed efforts of Mokoum persuaded the natives to venture a little farther: he felt sure that the caravan could not be more than five or six days' march from Lake Ngami, and once there, the animals could find pasturage and shade, and the men an abundance of fresh water. All these considerations he laid before the principal Bochjesmen. He showed them that it was really best to advance northwards. If they turned to the west, their march would be perilous, and to turn back was only to find the karroo desolate and dry. The natives at length yielded to his solicitations, and the almost exhausted caravan continued its course.

Happily this vast plain was in itself favourable to all astronomical observations, so that no delay arose from any natural obstruction. On one occasion there sprang up a sudden hope that nature was about to restore to them a supply of the water of which she had been so niggardly. A lagoon, a mile or two in extent, was discovered on the horizon. The reflection was indubitably of water, proving that what they saw was no mirage, due to the unequal density of the atmospheric strata. The caravan speedily turned in that direction, and the lagoon was reached towards five in the evening. Some of the horses broke away from their drivers, and galloped to the longed-for water. Having smelt it, they plunged in to their chests, but almost immediately returned to the bank. They had not drunk, and when the Bochjesmen arrived they found themselves by the side of a lagoon so impregnated with salt that its water could not be touched. Disappointment was keen, it was little short of despair. Mokoum thought that he should never induce the natives to proceed; but fortunately the only hope was in advancing, and even the natives were alive to the conviction that Lake Ngami was the nearest point where water could be procured. In four days, unless retarded by its labours, the expedition must reach the shores of the lake.

Every day was momentous. To economize time, Colonel Everest formed larger triangles and established fewer posts. No efforts were spared to hurry on the progress of the survey. Notwithstanding the application of every energy, the painful sojourn in the desert was prolonged, and it was not until the 21st of February that the level ground began to be rough and undulating. A mountain 500 or 600 feet high was descried about fifteen miles to the north-west. The bushman recognized it as Mount Scorzef, and, pointing to the north, said,—

" Lake Ngami is there."

" The Ngami! the Ngami!" echoed the natives, with noisy demonstration. They wished to hurry on in advance over the fifteen miles, but Mokoum restrained them, asserting that the country was infested by Makololos, and that it was important to keep together. Colonel Everest, himself eager to reach the lake, resolved to connect by a single triangle the station he was now occupying with Mount Scorzef. The instruments were therefore arranged, and the angle of the last triangle which had been already measured from the south was measured again from the station. Mokoum, in his impatience, only established a temporary camp; he hoped to reach the lake before night; but he neglected none of his usual precautions, and prudently sent out horsemen right and left to explore the underwood. Since the oryx-chase the Makololos seemed indeed to have abandoned their watch, still he would not incur any risk of being taken by surprise.

Thus carefully guarded by the bushman, the astronomers constructed their triangle. According to Emery's calculations it would carry them nearly to the twentieth parallel, the proposed limit of their arc. A few more triangles on the other side of Lake Ngami would complete their eighth degree; to verify the calculations, a new base would

"The Ngami! the Ngami!"—[Page 172.]

subsequently be measured directly on the ground, and the great enterprise would be ended. The ardour of the astronomers increased as they approached the fulfilment of their task.

Meanwhile there was considerable curiosity as to what the Russians on their side had accomplished. For six months the members of the commission had been separated, and it seemed probable to the English that the Russians had not suffered so much from heat and thirst, since their course had lain nearer Livingstone's route, and therefore in less arid regions. After leaving Kolobeng they would come across various villages to the right of their meridian, where they could easily revictual their caravan. But still it was not unlikely that in this less arid, though more frequented country, Matthew Strux's little band had been more exposed to the attacks of the plundering Makololos, and this was the more probable, since they seemed to have abandoned the pursuit of the English caravan.

Although the Colonel, ever engrossed, had no thought to bestow on these things, Sir John and Emery had often discussed the doings of their former comrades. They wondered whether they would come across them again, and whether they would find that they had obtained the same mathematical result as themselves, and whether the two computations of a degree in South Africa would be identical. Emery did not cease to entertain kind memories of his friend, knowing well that Zorn, for his part, would never forget him.

The measurement of the angles was now resumed. To obtain the angle at the station they now occupied, they had to observe two points of sight. One of these was formed by the conical summit of Mount Scorzef, and the other by a sharp peak three or four miles to the left of the meridian, whose direction was easily obtained by one of the telescopes of the repeating circle. Mount Scorzef was much more distant; its position would compel the observers to diverge considerably to the right of the meridian, but on examination they found they had no other choice. The station was therefore observed with the second telescope of the repeating circle, and the angular distance between Mount Scorzef and the smaller peak was obtained.

Notwithstanding the impatience of the natives, Colonel Everest, as calmly as though he were in his own observatory, made many successive registries from the graduated circle of his telescope, and then, by taking the average of all his readings, he obtained a result rigorously exact.

The day glided on, and it was not until the darkness prevented the reading of the instruments, that the Colonel brought his observations to an end, saying,—

"I am at your orders, Mokoum; we will start as soon as you like."

"And none too soon," replied Mokoum; "better had we accomplished our journey by daylight."

The proposal to start met with unanimous approval, and by seven o'clock the thirsty party were once more on the march.

Some strange foreboding seemed weighing on the mind of Mokoum, and he urged the three Europeans to look carefully to their rifles and to be well provided with ammunition. The night grew dark, the moon and stars were repeatedly veiled in mist, but the atmosphere near the ground was clear. The bushman's keen vision was ever watching the flanks and front of the caravan, and his unwonted disquietude could not fail to be noticed by Sir John, who was likewise on the watch. They toiled through the weary evening, occasionally stopping to gather together the loiterers, and at ten o'clock they were still six miles from the lake. The animals gasped for breath in an atmosphere so dry that the hygrometer could not have detected a trace of moisture.

Mokoum was indefatigable in his endeavours to keep the disorganized party close together; but, in spite of his remonstrances, the caravan no longer presented a compact nucleus. Men and beasts stretched out into a long file, and some oxen had sunk exhausted to the ground. The dismounted horsemen could hardly drag themselves along, and any stragglers could have been easily carried off by the smallest band of natives. Mokoum went in evident anxiety from one to another, and with word and gestures tried to rally the troop ; but his success was far from complete, and already, without his knowledge, some of his men were missing.

By eleven o'clock the foremost waggons were hardly more than three miles from their destination. In the gloom of night Mount Scorzef stood out distinctly in its solitary height, like an enormous pyramid, and the obscurity made its dimensions appear greater than they actually were. Unless Mokoum were mistaken, Lake Ngami lay just behind Mount Scorzef, so that the caravan must pass round its base in order to reach the tract of fresh water by the shortest route.

The bushman, in company with the three Europeans, took the lead, and prepared to turn to the left, when suddenly some distinct, though distant reports, arrested their attention. They reined in their horses, and listened with a natural anxiety. In a country where the natives use only lances and arrows the report of European fire-arms was rather startling. The Colonel and Sir John simultaneously asked the bushman from whence the sound could proceed. Mokoum asserted that he could perceive a light in the shadow at the summit of Mount Scorzef, and that he had no doubt that the Makololos were attacking a party of Europeans.

"Europeans!" cried Emery.

"Yes," replied Mokoum; "these reports can only be produced by European weapons."

"But what Europeans could they be?" began Sir John.

"Be who they may," broke in the Colonel, "we must go to their assistance."

"Yes; come on," said Emery, with no little excitement.

Before setting off for the mountain, Mokoum, for the last time, tried to rally the small band. But when the bushman turned round the caravan was dispersed, the horses unyoked, the waggons forsaken, and a few scattered shadows were flying along the plain towards the south.

"The cowards!" he cried; then turning to the English, he said, "Well, we must go on."

The Englishmen and the bushman, gathering up all the remaining strength of their horses, darted on to the north. After a while they could plainly distinguish the war-cry of the Makololos. Whatever was their number, it was evident they were making an attack on Mount Scorze, from the summit of which the flashes of fire continued Groups of men could be faintly distinguished ascending the sides. Soon the Colonel and his companions were on the rear of the besiegers. Abandoning their worn-out steeds, and shouting loud enough to be heard by the besieged, they fired at the mass of natives. The rapidity with which they re-loaded caused the Makololos to imagine themselves assailed by a large troop. The sudden attack surprised them, and, letting fly a shower of arrows and assagais, they retreated. Without losing a moment, the Colonel, Sir John, Emery, the bushman, and the sailors, never desisting from firing, darted among the group of natives, of whose bodies no less than fifteen soon strewed the ground.

The Makololos divided. The Europeans rushed into the gap, and, overpowering the foremost, ascended the slope backwards. In a few minutes they had reached the summit, which was now entirely in darkness, the besieged having suspended their fire for fear of injuring those who had come so opportunely to their aid.

They were the Russian astronomers. Strux, Palander, Zorn, and their five sailors, all were there: but of all the natives belonging to their caravan there remained but the faithful pioneer. The Bochjesmen had been as faithless to them as they had been to the English.

The instant the Colonel appeared, Strux darted from the top of a low wall that crowned the summit.

"The English!" he cried.

"Yes," replied the Colonel gravely; "but now neither Russian nor English. Nationalities be forgotten; for mutual defence we are kinsmen, in that we are one and all Europeans!"

The English come to the relief of the Russians. —[Page 178.]

CHAPTER XIX.

SCIENCE UNDAUNTED.

NOBLE words were those just uttered by the Colonel. In the face of the Makololos it was no time for hesitation or discussion, and English and Russians, forgetting their national quarrel, were now re-united for mutual defence more firmly than ever. Emery and Zorn had warmly greeted each other, and the others had sealed their new alliance with a grasp of the hand.

The first care of the English was to quench their thirst. Water, drawn from the lake, was plentiful in the Russian camp. Then, as soon as the Makololos were quiet enough to afford some respite, the astronomers, sheltered by a sort of casemate forming part of a deserted fortress, talked of all that had happened since their separation at Kolobeng.

It appeared that the same reason had brought the Russians so far to the left of their meridian as had caused the English to turn to the right of theirs. Mount Scorzef, halfway between the two arcs, was the only height in that district which would serve as a station on the banks of Lake Ngami. Each of the meridians crossed the lake, whose opposite shores it was necessary to unite trigonometrically by a large triangle. Naturally, therefore, the two rival expeditions met on the only mountain which could serve their purpose.

Matthew Strux then gave some details of his operations. After leaving Kolobeng, the Russian party had continued without irregularity. The old meridian, which had fallen by lot to the Russians, fell across a fertile and slightly undulated country, which offered every facility for the formation of the triangles. Like the English, they had suffered from the heat, but they had experienced no hardship from the want of water. Streams were abundant, and kept up a wholesome moisture. The horses and oxen had roamed over an immense pasturage, across verdant prairies broken by forests and underwood. The wild animals by night had been safely kept at a distance by sentinels and fires, nor had any natives been seen except those stationary in the villages in which Dr. Livingstone had always found a hospitable reception. All through the journey the Bochjesmen of the caravan had given no cause for complaint, nor was it until the previous day, when the Makololos to the number of 200 or 300 had appeared on the plain, that they had shown themselves faithless, and deserted. For thirty-six hours the expedition had now occupied the little fortress.

The Makololos had attacked them in the evening, after plundering the waggons left at the foot of the hill. The instruments fortunately, having been carried into the fort, were secure. The steamboat had also escaped the ravages of the natives; it had been immediately put together by the sailors, and was now at anchor in a little creek of Lake Ngami, behind the enormous rocks that formed the base of the mountain. Mount Scorzef sloped with sudden abruptness down to the lake, and there was no danger of an attack from that side.

Such was Matthew Strux's account. Colonel Everest, in his turn, related the incidents of his march, the fatigues and difficulties, and the revolt of the Bochjesmen, and it was found by comparison that the Russians had had a less harassing journey than their rivals.

The night of the 21st passed quietly. The bushman and sailors kept watch under the walls of the fort; the Makololos on their part did not renew any attack, but the bivouac-fires at the foot of the mountain proved that they had not relinquished their project. At daybreak the Europeans left their casemate for the purpose of reconnoitring the plain. The early morning light illumined the vast extent of country as far as the horizon. Towards the south lay the desert, with its burnt brown grass and barren aspect. Close under the mountain was the circular camp, containing a swarm of 400 to 500 natives. The fires were still alight, and some pieces of venison broiling on the hot embers. The encampment was something more than temporary; the Makololos were evidently determined not to abandon their prey. Either vengeance or an instinctive thirst for blood appeared to be prompting them, since all the valuables of both caravans, the waggons, horses, oxen, and provisions, had fallen into their power; or perhaps it might be that they coveted the fire-arms which the Europeans carried, and of which they made such terrible use. The united English and Russians held a long consultation with the bushman, and it was felt that they could not relax their watch until they should arrive at a definite decision. This decision must depend on a variety of circumstances, and first of all it was necessary to understand exactly the position of Mount Scorzef.

The mountain overlooked to the south, east, and west the vast desert which the astronomers, having traversed it, knew extended southwards to the karroo. In the west could be discerned the faint outlines of the hills bordering the fertile country of the Makololos, one of whose capitals, Maketo, lies about a hundred miles north-west of Lake Ngami. To the north the mountain commanded a country which was a great contrast to the arid steppes of the south. There were water, trees, and pasturage. For a hundred miles east and west lay the wide Lake Ngami, while from north to south its length was not more than 30 to 40 miles.

Beyond appeared a gentle, undulated country, enriched with forests and watered by the affluents of the Zambesi, and shut in to the extreme north by a low chain of mountains. This wide oasis was caused by the great artery, the Zambesi, which is to South Africa what the Danube is to Europe, or the Amazon to South America.

The side of the mountain towards the lake, steep as it was, was not so steep but that the sailors could accomplish an ascent and descent by a narrow way which passed from point to point. They thus contrived to reach the spot where the "Queen and Czar" lay hid, and, obtaining a supply of water, enabled the little garrison to hold out in the deserted fort as long as their provisions lasted.

The astronomers wondered why this little fort had been placed on the top of the mountain. Mokoum, who had visited the country as Livingstone's guide, explained that formerly the neighbourhood of Lake Ngami was frequented by traders in ivory and ebony. The ivory was furnished by the elephants and rhinoceroses; but the ebony trade was but too often another name for that traffic in human beings which is still carried on by the slave-traders in the region of the Zambesi. A great number of prisoners are made in the wars and pillages in the interior of the country, and these prisoners are sold as slaves. Mount Scorzef had been a centre of encampment for the ivory-traders, and it was there that they had been accustomed to rest before descending the Zambesi. They had fortified their position, to protect themselves and their slaves from depredations, since it was not an uncommon occurrence for the prisoners to be recaptured for fresh sale by the very men who had recently sold them. The route of the traders was now changed; they no longer passed the shores of the lake, and the little fort was falling into ruins. All that remained was an enclosure in the form of the sector of a circle, from the centre of which rose a small casemated redoubt, pierced with loop-holes, and surmounted by a small wooden turret.

But notwithstanding the condition of ruin into which it had fallen, the fortress offered the Europeans a welcome retreat. Behind the thick sandstone walls, and armed with their rapidly-loading guns, they were confident that they could keep back an army of Makololos, and, unless their provisions and ammunition failed, they would be able to complete their observations. At present they had plenty of ammunition; the coffer in which it was contained had been placed on the same waggon which carried the steam-boat, and had therefore escaped the rapacity of the natives. The great difficulty would be the possible failure of provisions. The Colonel and Strux made a careful inspection of the store, and found that there was only enough to last the eighteen men for two days. After a short breakfast, the astronomers and the bushman, leaving the sailors still to keep watch round the walls, assembled in the redoubt to discuss their situation.

"I cannot understand," said Mokoum, "why you are so uneasy. You say that we have only provisions for two days; but why stay here? Let us leave to-morrow, or even to-day. The Makololos need not hinder us; they could not cross the lake, and in the steamboat we may reach the northern shore in a few hours."

The astronomers looked at each other; the idea, natural as it was, had not struck them before. Sir John was the first to speak.

"But we have not yet completed the measurement of our meridian."

"Will the Makololos have any regard for your meridian?" asked the hunter.

"Very likely not," answered Sir John; "but *we* have a regard for it, and will not leave our undertaking incomplete. I am sure my colleagues agree with me."

"Yes," said the Colonel, speaking for all; "as long as one of us survives, and is able to put his eye to his telescope, the survey shall go on. If necessary, we will take our observations with our instrument in one hand and our gun in the other, even to the last extremity."

The energetic philosophers shouted out their resolution to proceed at every hazard.

When it was thus decided that the survey should at all risks be continued, the question arose as to the choice of the next station.

"Although there will be a difficulty," said Strux, "in joining Mount Scorzef trigonometrically to a station to the north of the lake, it is not impracticable. I have fixed on a peak in the extreme north-east, so that the side of the triangle will cross the lake obliquely."

"Well," said the Colonel, "if the peak exists, I do not see any difficulty."

"The only difficulty," replied Strux, "consists in the distance."

"What is the distance?"

"Over a hundred miles, and a lighted signal must be carried to the top of the peak."

"Assuredly that can be done," said the Colonel.

"And all that time, how are we to defend ourselves against the Makololos?" asked the bushman.

"We will manage that too."

Mokoum said that he would obey the Colonel's orders, and the conversation ended. The whole party left the casemate, and Strux pointed out the peak he had chosen. It was the conical peak of Volquiria, 300 feet high, and just visible in the horizon. Notwithstanding the distance, a powerful reflector could thence be discerned by means of a magnifying telescope, and the curvature of the earth's surface, which Strux had taken into account, would not be any obstacle. The real difficulty was how the lamp should be hoisted to the top of the mountain. The angle made at Mount Scorzef with Mount Volquiria and the preceding station would probably complete the measurement of the meridian, so that the operation was all important. Zorn and Emery offered to take this journey of a hundred miles in an unknown country, and, accompanied by the pioneer, prepared to start.

One of the canoes of birch-bark, which are manufactured by the natives with great dexterity, would be sufficient to carry them over the lake. Mokoum and the pioneer descended to the shore, where were growing some dwarf birches, and in a very short time had accomplished their task, and prepared the canoe.

At eight o'clock in the evening the newly-constructed craft was loaded with instruments, the apparatus for the reverberator, provisions, arms, and ammunition. It was arranged that the astronomers should meet again in a small creek known to both Mokoum and the pioneer; it was also agreed that as soon as the reverberator on Mount Volquiria should be perceived, Colonel Everest should light a signal on Mount Scorzef, so that Emery and Zorn, in their turn, might take the direction.

The young men took leave of their colleagues, and

descended the mountain in the obscurity of night, having been preceded by the pioneer and two sailors, one English and one Russian. The mooring was loosened, and the frail boat turned quietly across the lake.

On Guard on Mount Scorzef.—[Page 189.]

CHAPTER XX.

STANDING A SIEGE.

NOT without anxiety had the astronomers witnessed the departure of their young colleagues: they could not tell what dangers awaited them in that unknown country. Mokoum tried to reassure them by praising the courage of the pioneer, and besides, he said, the Makololos were too much occupied around Mount Scorzef to beat the country to the north of Lake Ngami. He instinctively felt that the Colonel and his party were in a more dangerous position than the two young astronomers.

The sailors and Mokoum kept watch in turns through the night. But "the reptiles," as the bushman termed the Makololos, did not venture another attack. They seemed to be waiting for reinforcements, in order to invade the mountain from all sides, and overcome by their numbers the resistance of the besieged.

The hunter was not mistaken in his conjectures; and when daylight appeared Colonel Everest perceived a sensible increase in the number of the natives. Their camp, carefully arranged round the base of the mountain, shut off escape on every side except that towards the lake. This side could not be invested, so that unless unforeseen circumstances occurred, retreat to the water was always practicable. But the Europeans had no thought of escaping: they occupied a post of honour, and were all agreed that it must not be abandoned. No allusion was ever made to the war between England and Russia, and both parties strove together to accomplish their scientific labour.

The interval of waiting for the signal on Mount Volquiria was employed in completing the measurement of the preceding triangle and in finding the exact latitude of Mount Scorzef by means of the altitudes of the stars.

Mokoum was called upon to say what would be the shortest possible space of time that must elapse before Emery and Zorn could reach Mount Volquiria. He replied that as the journey was to be performed on foot, and the country was continually crossed by rivers, he did not think that they could arrive in less than five days at least. They therefore adopted a maximum of six days, and portioned out their supplies to serve for that period. Their reserve was very limited, consisting only of a few pounds of biscuit, preserved meat, and pemmican, and had already been diminished by the portion furnished to the pioneer's little troop.

Colonel Everest and his companions, anxiously anticipating the sixth day, decided that the daily ration must be reduced to a third of their previous allowance. The thirteen men would doubtless suffer much from this small amount of nourishment, but there was an unflinching determination to bear up bravely.

"Besides," said Sir John, "we have room enough to hunt."

Mokoum shook his head doubtfully: he thought that game would be rare on the mountain. However, his gun need not be idle, and leaving the astronomers to examine and correct their registers, he set off with Sir John.

The Makololos were quietly encamped, and apparently patient in their intention of reducing the besieged by famine. The two hunters reconnoitred the mountain. The fort occupied a space of ground measuring not more than a quarter of a mile in its widest part. The soil was covered with flints and grass, dotted here and there with low shrubs, and bright with gladioli. Red heaths, silvery-leaved proteæ, and ericæ with wavy fronds, formed the flora of the mountain, and beneath the angles formed by the projections of rock sprung up thorny bushes ten feet high, with bunches of a sweet-smelling white flower. The bushman was ignorant of its name, but it was doubtless the *Arduina bispinosa*, which bears fruit like the barberry.

After an hour's search Sir John had seen no trace of game. Some little birds with dark wings and red beaks flew out of the bushes, but at the first shot they disappeared, no more to return. It was evident that the garrison must not depend on the products of the chase for sustenance.

"We can fish in the lake," said Sir John, standing and contemplating the fine extent of water.

"To fish without net or line," replied the bushman, "is as difficult as to lay hands on birds on the wing. But we will not despair; chance has hitherto favoured us."

"Chance! nay, not chance, but Providence," said Sir John. "That does not forsake us; it has brought us to the Russians, and will no doubt carry us on to our goal."

"And will Providence feed us, Sir John?" asked the bushman.

"No doubt, Mokoum," said Sir John encouragingly; and the bushman thought to himself that no blind trust in Providence should prevent him from using his own best exertions.

The 25th brought no change in the relative positions of besiegers and besieged. The Makololos, having brought in the plundered waggons, remained in their camp. Herds and flocks were grazing in the pasturages at the foot of the mountain, and some women and children, who had joined the tribe, went about and pursued their ordinary occupations. From time to time, some chief, recognizable by

An Attack on Mount Scorzef.—[Page 193.]

the richness of the skins which he wore, ascended the slope of the mountain and tried to examine the approaches to the summit; but the report of a rifle always took him speedily back to the plain. The Makololos then raised their war-cry, brandished their assagais, and all became quiet.

The following day the natives made a more serious attempt, and about fifty of them at once scaled three sides of the mountain. The whole garrison turned out to the foot of the enclosure, and the European arms caused considerable ravage among the Makololos. Five or six were killed, and the rest abandoned their project, but it was quite evident that if several hundred were to assault the mountain simultaneously, the besieged would find it difficult to face them on all sides. Sir John now thought of the mitrailleuse, which was the principal weapon of the "Queen and Czar," and proposed that it should be brought up to defend the front of the fortress. It was a difficult task to hoist the machine up the rocks, which in some parts were almost perpendicular; but the sailors showed themselves so agile and daring, that in the course of the day the mitrailleuse was installed in the embrasure of the embattled enclosure. Thence, its twenty-five muzzles, arranged in the shape of a fan, would cover the front of the fort, and the natives would thus early make acquaintance with the engine of death which in after-years was to effect such devastation amongst the civilized armies of the European continent.

The dry air and clear sky had enabled the astronomers each night to pursue their observations. They had found the latitude of Mount Scorzef to be 19°, 37′, which result confirmed their opinion that they were less than half a degree from the northern extremity of their meridian, and that consequently the next triangle would complete the series.

The night passed without any fresh alarm. If circumstances had favoured the pioneer, he and his companions would reach Mount Volquiria the following day, so that the astronomers kept unflagging watch through the next night for the appearance of the light. Strux and the Colonel had already pointed the telescope to the peak, so that it was continuously embraced in the field of the object-glass, otherwise it would have been difficult to discern on a dark night; as it was, the light would doubtless be perceived immediately on its appearance.

All day Sir John beat fruitlessly the bushes and long grass. He could not unearth a single animal that was fit to eat. The very birds, disturbed from their retreats, had gone to the underwood on the shore for shelter. Sir John was extremely vexed, inasmuch as he was not hunting merely for personal gratification, but to supply the necessities of the party. Perhaps he himself suffered from hunger more than his three colleagues, whose attention was more riveted by their application to science. The sailors and Mokoum suffered equally with Sir John. One more day and their scanty reserve would be at an end, and if the pioneer's expedition were delayed, they would soon be exposed to a severe extremity of hunger,

The dark, calm night was passed in watching; but the horizon remained wrapped in shade, and no light appeared in the object-glass of the telescope. The minimum of time, however, allowed to the expedition had hardly expired, and they felt that they were bound to exhibit patience for a while.

The next day the garrison ate their last morsel of meat and biscuit; but their courage did not fail, and, though they should be obliged to feed on what herbs they could gather, they were resolved to hold out.

The succeeding night passed without any result. More than once the astronomers believed that they had seen the light, but it was always proved to be a star in the misty horizon.

On the 1st of March they were compelled absolutely to fast. Having been for some time accustomed to meagre and inadequate nourishment, they passed the first day without much acute suffering, but on the morrow they began to experience the pangs of craving. Sir John and Mokoum, haggard-eyed, and sensitive to the gnawings of hunger, wandered over the top of the mountain; but no game whatever was to be seen. They began to think that, as the Colonel had said, they should literally have to feed on grass. If they only had the stomachs of ruminants, thought poor Sir John, as he eyed the abundant pasturage, they would be able to hold out; but still no game, still not even a bird! He gazed intently over the lake, in which the sailors had fished in vain; and it was impossible to get near the wary aquatic birds that skimmed the tranquil waters.

At last, worn out with fatigue, Sir John and his companion lay down on the grass at the foot of a mound of earth some five or six feet high. Here they fell, not precisely into a sleep, but into a heavy torpor, which for a while benumbed their sufferings. How long this drowsiness would have lasted neither of them could have said; but in about an hour Sir John was aroused by a disagreeable pricking. He tried to slumber again, but the pricking continued, and at last impatiently he opened his eyes.

He was entirely covered, face, hands, and clothes, with swarms of white ants. He started to his feet, and his sudden movement aroused the bushman, who was covered in the same way. But to Sir John's great surprise, the bushman, instead of shaking off the insects, carried them by handfuls to his mouth, and devoured them greedily. Sir John's first sensation was disgust at his voracity.

The Rice of the Bochjesmen.—[Page 196.]

"Come, eat, do as I do!" said the bushman; "it is the rice of the Bochjesmen."

And that was, in truth, the native term for these insects. The Bochjesmen feed on both the black and white species, but they consider the white to be of superior quality. The only drawback is, that they must be swallowed in large quantities to satisfy any longing for food. The Africans generally mix them with the gum of the mimosa, thus rendering them capable of affording a less unsubstantial meal; but as the mimosa did not grow on Mount Scorzef, the bushman had to content himself with his rice *au naturel.*

Sir John, in spite of his repugnance, resolved to imitate him. The insects poured forth by thousands from their enormous ant-hill, which was none other than the mound of earth by which the weary sufferers had reclined. Sir John took them by handfuls, and carried them to his lips; he did not dislike the flavour, which was a grateful acid; and gradually he felt his hunger moderated.

Mokoum did not forget his companions in misfortune. He ran to the fort, and brought out the garrison. The sailors were without difficulty induced to attack the singular food, and although the astronomers hesitated a moment, yet, encouraged by Sir John's example, and half dead with inanition, they soon at least assuaged the intenseness of their hunger by devouring considerable quantities of these ants.

But an unexpected incident procured for the starving men a more solid meal. In order to lay in a provision of the insects, Mokoum resolved to destroy one side of the enormous ant-hill. It consisted of a central conical mound, with smaller cones arranged at intervals round its base. The hunter had already made several blows with his hatchet, when a singular grunting sound from the centre attracted his attention: he paused in his work of destruction, and listened, while his companions watched him in silence. He struck a few more blows, and the groan was repeated more audibly than before. The bushman rubbed his hands, whilst his eyes evidently sparkled. Once more attacking the ant-hill, he opened a cavity about a foot wide. The ants were escaping on every side; but of them he took no heed, leaving the sailors to collect them in sacks. All at once a strange animal appeared at the mouth of the hole. It was a quadruped with a long snout, small mouth, and flexible tongue, which protruded to a great length; its ears were straight, its legs short, and its tail long and pointed. Long grey bristles with a reddish tinge covered its lank body, and its feet were armed with enormous claws. Mokoum killed it at once with a sharp blow on the snout. "There is our supper," he said. "It has been some time coming, but it will not taste the worse for that. Now for a fire, and a ramrod for a spit, and we will feast as we have never feasted in our lives."

The bushman speedily began to skin the animal, which was a species of octeropus or ant-eater, very common in South Africa, and known to the Dutch at the Cape under the name of "earth-pig." Swarms of ants are devoured by this creature, which catches them by means of its long glutinous tongue.

The meal was soon cooked; perhaps it would have been better for a few more turns of the spit, but the hungry men were impatient. The firm, wholesome flesh was declared to be excellent, although slightly impregnated with the acid of the ants

After the repast the Europeans felt re-invigorated, and animated with more steadfast purpose to persevere; and in truth there was need of encouragement. All through the following night no light appeared on Mount Volquiria.

CHAPTER XXI.

SUSPENSE.

It was now the ninth day since Zorn and Emery had started on their expedition. Their colleagues, detained on the summit of Mount Scorzef, began to give way to the fear that they had fallen into some irretrievable misfortune. They were all well aware that the young astronomers would omit nothing that lay in their power to ensure the success of their enterprise, and they dreaded lest their courageous spirit should have exposed them to danger, or betrayed them into the hands of the wandering tribes. They waited always impatiently for the moment when the sun sank behind the horizon, that they might begin their nightly watch, and then all their hopes seemed concentrated on the field of their telescope.

All through the 3rd of March, wandering up and down the slopes, hardly exchanging a word, they suffered as they had never suffered before; not even the heat and fatigues of the desert, nor the tortures of thirst, had equalled the pain that arose from their apprehensions. The last morsel of the ant-eater had been devoured, and nothing now remained but the insufficient nourishment afforded by the ants.

Night came, dark and calm, and extremely favourable to their operations; but although the Colonel and Strux watched alternately with the utmost perseverance, no light appeared, and the sun's rays soon rendered any longer observations futile.

There was still nothing immediate to fear from the Makololos; they seemed resolved to reduce the besieged by famine, and it seemed hardly likely that they would desist from their project. The unhappy Europeans were tortured afresh with hunger, and could only diminish their sufferings by devouring the bulbs of the gladioli that sprang up between the rocks.

Yet they were hardly prisoners; their detention was voluntary. At any moment the steamboat would have carried them to a fertile land, where game and fruit abounded. Several times they discussed the propriety of sending Mokoum to the northern shore to hunt for the little garrison; but this manœuvre might be discovered by the natives; and there would be a risk to the steam-vessel, and consequently to the whole party, in the event of finding other hostile tribes to the north of the lake: accordingly the proposal was rejected, and it was decided that they must abide in company, and that all or none must depart. To leave Mount Scorzef before the observations were complete was an idea that was not entertained for a moment; the astronomers were determined to wait patiently until the faintest hope of success should be extinguished.

"We are no worse off," remarked the Colonel in the course of the day to his assembled companions, "than Arago, Biot, and Rodriguez were when they were measuring the arc from Dunkirk to Ivica: they were uniting the Spanish coast and the island by a triangle of which the sides were more than eighty miles long. Rodriguez was installed on an isolated peak, and kept up lighted lamps at night, while the French astronomers lived in tents a hundred miles away in the desert of Las Palmas. For sixty nights Arago and Biot watched for the signal, and, discouraged at last, were about to renounce their labour, when, on the sixty-first night, appeared a light, which it was impossible to confound with a star. Surely, gentlemen, if those French astronomers could watch for sixty-one nights in the interests of science, we English and Russians must not give up at the end of nine."

The Colonel's companions most heartily approved the sentiment; but they could have said that Arago and Biot did not endure the tortures of hunger during their long vigil.

In the course of the day Mokoum perceived an unusual agitation in the Makololo camp. He thought at first that they were about to raise the siege, but, after some contemplation, he discovered that their intentions were evidently hostile, and that they would probably assault the mountain in the course of the night. All the women and children, under the protection of a few men, left the encampment, and turned eastward to the shores of the lake. It was probable that the natives were about to make a last attack on the fortress before retiring finally to Maketo. The bushman communicated his opinion to the Europeans. They resolved to keep a closer watch all night, and to have their guns in readiness. The enclosure of the fort was broken in several places, and as the number of the natives was now largely increased they would find no difficulty in forcing their way through the gaps. Colonel Everest therefore thought it prudent to have the steamboat in readiness for a retreat. The engineer received orders to light the fire, but not until sunset, lest the smoke should reveal the presence of the vessel to the natives; and to keep up the steam, in order to start at the first signal. The evening repast was composed of white ants and gladiolus bulbs—a meagre supper for men about to fight with several hundred savages; but they were resolute, and staunchly awaited the engagement which appeared imminent.

Towards six o'clock, when night was coming on with its tropical celerity, the engineer descended the mountain, and proceeded to light the fire of the steamboat. It was still the Colonel's intention not to effect an escape until the last extremity: moreover, he was firm in his determination to abide until the night was advanced, that he might give himself the last chance of observing the signal from Mount Volquiria. The sailors were placed at the foot of the rampart, with orders to defend the breaches to the last. All arms were ready, and the mitrailleuse, armed with the heaviest ammunition that they had in store, spread its formidable mouth across the embrasure.

For several hours the Colonel and Strux, posted in the narrow donjon, kept a constant watch on the peak of Volquiria. The horizon was dark, while the finest of the southern constellations were resplendent in the zenith. There was no wind, and not a sound broke the imposing stillness of nature. The bushman, however, posted on a projection of rock, heard sounds which gradually became more distinct. He was not mistaken; the Makololos were at length commencing their assault on the mountain.

Until ten o'clock the assailants did not move; their fires were extinguished, and camp and plain were alike wrapped in obscurity. Suddenly Mokoum saw shadows moving up the mountain, till the besiegers seemed but a few hundred feet from the plateau on which stood the fort.

"Now then, quick and ready!" cried Mokoum.

The garrison immediately advanced to the south side of the fort, and opened a running fire on the assailants. The

Watching for the Signal from Mount Volquiria.—[Page 204.]

Makololos answered by a war-cry, and, in spite of the firing, continued to advance. In the light caused by the flash of the guns, the Europeans perceived such swarms of natives that resistance seemed impossible. But still they trusted that their well-directed balls were doing considerable execution, and they discerned that not a few of the natives were rolling down the sides of the mountain. Hitherto, however, nothing arrested them: with savage cries they continued to press on in compacted order, without even waiting to hurl a single dart. Colonel Everest put himself at the head of his little troop, who seconded him admirably, not excepting Palander, who probably was handling a gun for almost the first time. Sir John, now on one rock now on another, sometimes kneeling sometimes lying, did wonders, and his gun, heated with the rapidity of the repeated loading, began to burn his hands. Mokoum, as ever, was patient, bold, and undaunted in his confidence.

But the valour and precision of the besieged could avail nothing against the torrent of numbers. Where one native fell, he was replaced by twenty more, and, after a somewhat prolonged opposition, Colonel Everest felt that he must be overpowered. Not only did the natives swarm up the south slope of the mountain, but they made an ascent also by the side slopes. They did not hesitate to use the dead bodies of the fallen as stepping-stones, and they even lifted them up, and sheltered themselves behind them, as they mounted. The scene revealed by the flash of the fire-arms was appalling, and the Europeans saw enough to make them fully aware that they could expect no quarter, and that they were being assaulted by barbarians as savage as tigers.

At half-past ten the foremost natives had reached the plateau. The besieged, who were still uninjured (the natives not yet having employed their arrows and assagais), were thoroughly conscious they were impotent to carry on a combat hand to hand. The Colonel, in a calm, clear voice that could be heard above the tumult, gave the order to retire. With a last discharge the little band withdrew behind the walls. Loud cries greeted their retreat, and the natives immediately made a nearer approach in their attempt to scale the central breach.

A strange and unlooked for reception awaited them. Suddenly at first, and subsequently repeated at intervals but of a few minutes, there was a growling reverberation as of rolling thunder. The sinister sound was the report of the exploding mitrailleuse, which Sir John had been prepared to employ, and now worked with all his energy. Its twenty-five muzzles spread over a wide range, and the balls, continually supplied by a self-adjusting arrangement, fell like hail among the assailants. The natives, swept down at each discharge, responded at first with a howl and then with a harmless shower of arrows.

"She plays well," said the bushman, approaching Sir John. "When you have played your tune, let me play mine."

But there was no need for Sir John to be relieved; the mitrailleuse was soon silent. The Makololos were struck with consternation, and had sought shelter from the torrent of grape-shot, having retired under the flanks of the fort, leaving the plateau strewn with numbers of their dead.

In this instant of respite the Colonel and Strux regained the donjon, and there, collecting themselves to a composure as complete as if they were under the dome of an observatory, they kept a constant eye upon their telescope, and scanned the peak of Volquiria. When, after a short period of rest, the yells of the Makololos made them aware that the combat was renewed, they only persevered in their determination, and resolved that they would alternately remain to guard their invaluable instrument.

The combat, in truth, had been renewed, The range of the mitrailleuse was inadequate to reach all the natives, who, uttering their cries of mortal vengeance, rallied again, and swarmed up every opening. The besieged, protected by their fire-arms, defended the breaches foot by foot; they had only received a few scratches from the points of the assagais, and were able to continue the fight for half an hour with unabated ardour.

Towards half-past eleven, while the Colonel was in the

thick of the fray, in the middle of an angry fusillade, Matthew Strux appeared at his side. His eye was wild and radiant: an arrow had just pierced his hat and quivered above his head.

"The signal! the signal!" he cried.

The Colonel was incredulous, but ascertaining the correctness of the welcome announcement, discharged his rifle for the last time, and with an exuberant shout of rejoicing, rushed towards the donjon, followed by his intrepid colleague. There, kneeling down, he placed his eye to the telescope, and perceived with the utmost delight the signal, so long delayed and yet so patiently expected.

It was truly a marvellous sight to see these two astronomers work during the tumult of the conflict. The natives had by their numbers forced the enclosure, and Sir John and the bushman were contending for every step. The Europeans fought with their balls and hatchets, while the Makololos responded with their arrows and assagais.

Meanwhile the Colonel and Strux intently continued their observations, and Palander, equally composed, noted down their oft-repeated readings. More than once an arrow grazed their head, and broke against the inner wall of the donjon. But their eye was ever fixed on the signal, and reading the indications of the vernier, they incessantly verified each other's calculations.

"Only once more," said Strux, sliding the telescope along

the graduated scale. An instant later, and it would have been too late for any observations, but the direction of the light was calculated to the minutest fraction of a second ; and at that very instant an enormous stone, hurled by a native, sent the register flying from Palander's hands, and smashed the repeating-circle.

They must now fly in order to save the result which they had obtained at the cost of such continuous labour. The natives had already penetrated the casemate, and might at any moment appear in the donjon. The Colonel and his colleagues caught up their guns, and Palander his precious register, and all escaped through one of the breaches. Their companions, some slightly wounded, were ready to cover their retreat, but just as they were about to descend the north side of the mountain, Strux remembered that they had failed to kindle the signal. In fact, for the completion of the survey, it was necessary that the two astronomers on Mount Volquiria should in their turn observe the summit of Mount Scorzef, and were doubtless anxiously expecting the answering light.

The Colonel recognized the imperative necessity for yet one more effort, and whilst his companions, with almost superhuman energy, repulsed the natives, he re-entered the donjon. This donjon was formed of an intricate framework of dry wood, which would readily ignite by the application of a flame. The Colonel set it alight with the powder from the priming of his gun, and, rushing out, rejoined his companions. In a few moments, rolling their mitrailleuse before them, the Europeans, under a shower of arrows and various missiles, were descending the mountain, and, in their turn, driving back the natives with a deadly fire, reached the steamboat. The engineer, according to orders, had kept up the steam. The mooring was loosened, the screw set in motion, and the "Queen and Czar" advanced rapidly over the dark waters. They were shortly far enough out to see the summit of the mountain. The donjon was blazing like a beacon, and its light would be easily discerned from the peak of Volquiria. A resounding cheer of triumph from English and Russians greeted the bonfire they had left behind.

Emery and Zorn would have no cause for complaint; they had exhibited the twinkling of a star, and had been answered by the glowing of a sun.

The Steamboat leaving Mount Scorzef.—[Page 210.]

CHAPTER XXII.

HIDE AND SEEK.

WHEN daylight re-appeared, the vessel was nearing the northern shore of the lake. There was no trace of natives, consequently the Colonel and his companions, who had been ready armed, laid aside their guns as the "Queen and Czar" drew up in a little bay hollowed in the rocks. The bushman, Sir John, and one of the sailors set out at once to reconnoitre the neighbourhood. They could perceive no sign of Makololos, and fortunately they found game in abundance. Troops of antelopes grazed in the long grass and in the shelter of the thickets, and a number of aquatic birds frequented the shores of the lake. The hunters returned with ample provision, and the whole party could enjoy the savoury venison, a supply of which was now unlikely to fail them again.

The camp was arranged under the great willows near the lake, on the banks of a small river. The Colonel and Strux had arranged to meet on the northern shore with the pioneer's little party, and the rest afforded by the few days of expectation was gratefully enjoyed by all. Palander employed himself in rectifying and adjusting the results of the latest observations, while Mokoum and Sir John hunted most vigorously over the fertile, well-watered country, abounding in game, of which the Englishman would have been delighted, had it been in his power, to complete a purchase on behalf of the British government. Three days after, on the 8th of March, some gun-shots announced the arrival of the remainder of the party for whom they tarried. Emery, Zorn, the two sailors, and the pioneer, were all in perfect health. Their theodolite, the only instrument remaining to the Commission, was safe. The young astronomers and their companions were received with joyous congratulations. In a few words they related that their journey had not been devoid of difficulty. For two days they had lost their way in the forests that skirted the mountainous district, and with only the vague indications of the compass they would never have reached Mount Volquiria, if it had not been for the shrewd intelligence of the pioneer. The ascent of the mountain was rough, and the delay had caused the young astronomers as much impatience as it had their colleagues on Mount Scorzef. They had carefully, by barometrical observations, calculated that the summit of Volquiria was 3200 feet above the level of the sea. The light, increased by a strong reflector, was first lighted on the night of the 4th; thus the observers on

Mount Scorzef had perceived it as soon as it appeared. Emery and Zorn had easily discerned the intense fire caused by the burning fortress, and with the theodolite had completed the measurement of the triangle.

"And did you determine the latitude of the peak?" said the Colonel to Emery.

"Yes, most accurately," replied Emery; "we found it to be 19° 37′ 35.337″."

"Well, gentlemen," said the Colonel, "we may say that our task is ended. We have measured, by means of sixty-three triangles, an arc of more than eight degrees in length; and when we have rigidly corrected our results, we shall know the exact value of the degree, and consequently of the *mètre*, in this part of the globe."

A cheer of satisfaction could not be repressed amongst the others.

"And now," added the Colonel, "we have only to descend the Zambesi in order to reach the Indian Ocean: is it not so, Mr Strux?"

"It is so," answered Strux; "but I think we ought still to adopt some means of testing our previous operations. Let us continue our triangles until we find a place suitable for the direct measurement of a base. The agreement between the lengths of the base, obtained by the calculations and by the direct measurement, will alone tell what degree of accuracy we ought to attribute to our observations."

Strux's proposition was unanimously adopted. It was agreed to construct a series of subsidiary triangles until a side could be measured with the platinum rods. The steamboat, descending the affluents of the Zambesi, was to await the travellers below the celebrated Victoria Falls. Every thing being arranged, the little troop, with the exception of four sailors on board the "Queen and Czar," started the next day at sunrise. Some stations had been chosen to the east and the angles measured, and along this favourable country, they hoped easily to accomplish their auxiliary series. The bushman had adroitly caught a quagga, of which, willing or unwilling, he made a beast of burden to carry the theodolite, the measuring-rods, and some other luggage of the caravan.

The journey proceeded rapidly. The undulated country afforded many points of sight for the small accessory triangles. The weather was fine, and it was not needful to have recourse to nocturnal observations. The travellers could nearly always find shelter in the woods, and, besides, the heat was not insufferable, since some vapours arose from the pools and streams which tempered the sun's rays. Every want was supplied by the hunters, and there was no longer any thing to be feared from the natives, who seemed to be more to the south of Lake Ngami.

Matthew Strux and the Colonel seemed to have forgotten all their personal rivalry, and although there was no close intimacy between them, they were on the most perfect terms of courtesy.

Day after day, during a period of three weeks, the observations steadily proceeded. For the measurement of a base the astronomers required a tract of land that should be level for several miles, and the very undulations of the soil that were desirable for the establishment of the points of sight were unfavourable for that observation. They proceeded to the north-east, sometimes following the right bank of the Cnobi, one of the principal tributaries of the Upper Zambesi, in order to avoid Maketo, the chief settlement of the Makololos. They had now every reason to anticipate that their return would be happily accomplished, and that no further natural obstacle would occur, and they hoped that their difficulties were all at an end. The country which they were traversing was comparatively well known and they could not be far from the villages of the Zambesi which Livingstone had lately visited. They thus thought with reason that all the most arduous part of their task was over, when an incident, of which the consequences might have been serious, almost compromised the result of the whole expedition.

Nicholas Palander was the hero, or rather was nearly being the victim, of the adventure.

The intrepid but thoughtless calculator, unwarned by his escape from the crocodiles, had still the habit of withdrawing himself from his companions. In an open country there was no great danger in this, but in woods Palander's abstraction might lead to serious consequences. Strux and the bushman gave him many warnings, and Palander, though much astonished at what he considered an excess of prudence, promised to conform to their wishes.

On the 27th, some hours had passed since Strux and Mokoum had seen any thing of Palander. The little troop were travelling through thickets of low trees and shrubs, extending as far as the horizon. It was important to keep together, as it would be difficult to discover the track of any one lost in the wood. But seeing and fearing nothing, Palander, who had been posted, pencil in one hand, the register in the other, on the left flank of the troop, was not long in disappearing.

When, towards four o'clock, Strux and his companions found that Palander was no longer with them, they became extremely anxious. His former aberrations were still fresh in their remembrance, and it was probably the abstracted calculator alone by whom they had been forgotten. The march was stopped, and they all shouted in vain. The bushman and the sailors dispersed for a quarter of a mile in each direction, beating the bushes, trampling through the woods and long grass, firing off their guns, but yet without success. They became still more uneasy, especially Matthew Strux, to whose anxiety was joined an extreme

Palander robbed by the Chacma,—[Page 217.]

irritation against his unlucky colleague. This was not the first time that Palander had served them thus, and if the Colonel had laid any blame on him, Strux would not have known what to say. Under the circumstances, the only thing to be done was to encamp in the wood, and begin a more careful search.

The Colonel and his companions had just arranged to place their camp near a glade of considerable extent, when a cry, unlike any thing human, resounded at some distance to the left. Almost immediately, running at full speed, appeared Palander. His head was bare, his hair dishevelled, and his clothes torn in some parts almost to rags. His companions plied him with questions; but the unhappy man, with haggard and distended eye, whose compressed nostrils still further hindered his short jerking respiration, could not bring out a word.

What had happened? why had he wandered away? and why did he appear so terrified? At last, to their repeated questions, he gasped out, in almost unintelligible accents, something about the registers.

The astronomers shuddered; the registers, on which was inscribed every result of their operations, and which the calculator had never allowed out of his possession, even when asleep, these registers were missing. No matter whether Palander had lost them, or whether they had been stolen from him; they were gone, and all their labour was in vain!

While his companions, mutely terrified, only looked at each other, Matthew Strux could no longer restrain his anger. He burst forth into all manner of invective against the miserable man, threatening him with the displeasure of the Russian government, and adding, that if he did not suffer under the knout he should linger out his life in Siberia.

To all this Palander answered but by a movement of the head: he seemed to acquiesce in all these condemnations, and even thought the judgment would be too lenient.

"But perhaps he has been robbed," said the Colonel at last.

"What matters?" cried Strux, beside himself; "what business had he so far away from us, after our continual warning?"

"True," replied Sir John, "but we ought to know whether he has lost the registers or been robbed of them. Has any one robbed you, Palander?" continued he, turning to the poor man, who had sunk down with fatigue.

Palander made a sign of affirmation.

"Who?" continued Sir John. "Natives? Makololos?"

Palander shook his head.

"Well, then, Europeans?" asked Sir John.

"No," answered Palander in a stifled voice.

"Who then?" shouted Strux, shaking his clenched fists in Palander's face.

"They were neither natives—nor white men—but monkeys," stammered out Palander at last.

It was a fact that the unhappy man had been robbed by a monkey, and if the consequences of the incident had been less serious, the whole party would have broken out into laughter. Mokoum explained that what had just happened was of frequent occurrence. Many times, to his knowledge, had travellers been rifled by these pig-headed chacmas, a species of baboon very common in South African forests. The calculator had been plundered by these animals, though not without a struggle, as his ragged garments testified. Still, in the judgment of his companions, there was no excuse to be made: if he had remained in his proper place this irreparable loss would not have occurred.

"We did not take the trouble," began Colonel Everest, "to measure an arc of meridian in South Africa for a blunderer like you—"

He did not finish his sentence, conscious that it was useless to continue to abuse the unhappy man, whom Strux had not ceased to load with every variety of vituperation. The Europeans were, without exception, quite overpowered by emotion; but Mokoum, who was less sensitive to the importance of the loss, retained his self-possession.

"Perhaps even yet," he said, "something may be done to assist you in your perplexity. These chacmas are always careful of their stolen goods, and if we find the robber we shall find the registers with him. But time is precious, and none must be lost."

The bushman had opened a ray of hope. Palander revived at the suggestion: he arranged his tattered clothes as best he could, and having accepted the jacket of one sailor and the hat of another, declared himself ready to lead his companions to the scene of his adventure.

They all started off towards the west, and passed the night and the ensuing day without any favourable result. In many places, by traces on the ground and the bark of the trees, the bushman and the pioneer recognized unmistakable vestiges of the baboons, of which Palander affirmed that he was sure he had seen no less than ten. The party was soon on their track, and advanced with the utmost precaution, the bushman affirming that he could only count on success in his search by taking the chacmas by surprise, since they were sagacious animals, such as could only be approached by some device of secrecy.

Early the following morning one of the Russian sailors, who was somewhat in front, perceived, if not the actual thief, yet one of its associates. He prudently returned to the little troop, who came at once to a halt. The Europeans, who had resolved to obey Mokoum in every thing, awaited his instructions. The bushman begged them to remain in quietness where they were, and, taking Sir John and the pioneer, turned towards the part of the wood already visited by the sailor, carefully keeping under shelter of the trees and bushwood.

In a short time the bushman and his two companions caught sight of one chacma, and almost immediately of nine or ten more, gambolling among the branches. Crouching behind a tree, they attentively watched the animals. Their long tails were continually sweeping the ground, and their powerful muscles, sharp teeth, and pointed claws, rendered them formidable even to the beasts of prey. These chacmas are the terror of the Boers, whose fields of corn and maize, and occasionally whose habitations, are plundered by them.

Not one of the animals had as yet espied the hunters. but they all continued their sport, yelping and barking as though they were great ill-favoured dogs. The important point for determination was, whether the actual purloiner of the missing documents was there. All doubt was put aside when the pioneer pointed out a chacma wrapped in a rag of Palander's coat. Sir John felt that this creature must be secured at any price, but he was obliged to act with great circumspection, aware as he was that a single false movement would cause the whole herd to decamp at once.

"Stay here," said Mokoum to the pioneer; "Sir John and I will return to our companions, and set about surrounding the animals; but meanwhile do not lose sight of them.

The pioneer remained at his post, while Sir John and the bushman returned to Colonel Everest. The only means of securing the suspected culprit was to surround the whole troop. To accomplish this, the Europeans divided into separate detachments; one composed of Strux, Emery, Zorn, and three sailors, was to join the pioneer, and to form a semicircle around him; and the other, comprising the Colonel, Mokoum, Sir John, Palander, and the other three sailors, made a *détour* to the left, in order to fall back upon the herd from the other side

Implicitly following the bushman's advice, they all advanced with the utmost caution. Their guns were ready, and it was agreed that the chacma with the rags should be the aim for every shot.

Mokoum kept a watchful eye upon Palander, and insisted upon his marching close to himself, lest his unguardedness should betray him into some fresh folly. The worthy astronomer was almost beside himself in consternation at his loss, and evidently thought it a question of life or death.

After marching with the frequent halts which the policy of being unobserved suggested, and continuing to diverge for half an hour, the bushman considered that they might now fall back. He and his companions, each about twenty paces apart, advanced like a troop of Pawnies on a war-trail, without a word or gesture, avoiding even the least rustling in the branches. Suddenly the bushman stopped; the rest instantly followed his example, and standing with their finger on the lock of their guns, were ready to raise them to their shoulder. The band of chacmas was in sight, they were already sensible of some danger, and seemed on the look-out. The great animal which had stolen the registers had, to their fancy, an appearance of being especially agitated. It had been already recognized by Palander, who muttered something like an imprecation between his teeth.

The chacma looked as if it was making signs to its companions: some females, with their young ones on their shoulders, had collected in a group, and the males went to and fro around them. The hunters still drew on, one and all keeping a steady eye direct towards the ostensible thief. All at once, by an involuntary movement, Palander's gun went off in his hands. Sir John broke out into an exclamation of disgust, and instantly afterwards fired. Ten reports followed: three chacmas lay dead on the ground, and the rest, with a prodigious bound, passed over the hunters' heads.

The robber baboon alone remained: it darted at the trunk of a sycamore, which it climbed with an amazing agility, and disappeared among the branches. The bushman, having keenly surveyed the spot, asserted that the registers were there concealed, and fearing lest the chacma should escape across the trees, he calmly aimed and fired. The animal, wounded in the leg, fell from branch to branch. In one of its fore-claws it was seen to clutch the registers, which it had taken from a fork of the tree.

At the sight, Palander, with a leap like a chamois, darted at the chacma, and a tremendous struggle ensued. The cries of both man and beast mingled in harsh and discordant strain, and the hunters dared not take aim at the chacma for fear of wounding their comrade. Strux, beside himself with rage, shouted again and again that they should fire, and in his furious agitation he would probably have done so, if it had not been that he was accidentally without a cartridge for his gun, which had been already discharged.

The combat continued; sometimes Palander, sometimes the chacma, was uppermost. The astronomer, his shoulders lacerated by the creature's claws, tried to strangle his adversary. At last the bushman, seizing a favourable moment, made a sudden dash, and killed the ape with one blow of his hatchet.

Nicholas Palander, bleeding, exhausted, and insensible, was picked up by his colleagues: in his last effort he had recaptured his registers, which he was found unconsciously grasping to his bosom.

The carcase of the chacma was conveyed with glee to the camp. At the evening repast it furnished a delicious meal to the hunters. To all of them, but especially to Palander, not only had the excitement of the chase quickened their appetite for the palatable dish, but the relish was heightened by the gratifying knowledge that vengeance was satisfied.

Palander's Combat with the Chacma.—[Page 224.]

CHAPTER XXIII.

HOMEWARD BOUND.

PALANDER'S wounds were not serious : the bushman dressed the contused limbs with herbs, and the worthy astronomer, sustained by his triumph, was soon able to travel. Any exuberance on his part, however, was of short duration, and he quickly became again engrossed in his world of figures. He only now retained one of the registers, because it had been thought prudent that Emery should take possession of the other. Under the circumstances, Palander made the surrender with entire good-humour.

The operation of seeking a plain suitable for a base was now resumed. On the 1st of April the march was somewhat retarded by wide marshes; to these succeeded numerous pools, whose waters spread a pestilential odour; but, by forming larger triangles, Colonel Everest and his companions soon escaped the unhealthy region.

The whole party were in excellent spirits. Zorn and Emery

often congratulated themselves on the apparent concord that existed between their chiefs. Zorn one day expressed his hope to his friend that when they returned to Europe they would find that peace had been concluded between England and Russia, so that they might remain as good friends as they had been in Africa.

Emery replied that he acquiesced entirely in the hope: in days when war is seldom long protracted they might be sanguine all would be terminated by the date of their return.

Zorn had already understood from Emery that it was not his intention to return immediately to the Cape, and expressed his hope that he might introduce him to the observatory at Kiew. This proposal Emery expressed his desire to embrace, and added that he should indulge the expectation that Zorn would at some future time visit the Cape.

With these mutual assignations they made their plans for future astronomical researches, ever reiterating their hopes that the war would be at an end.

"Anyhow," observed Emery, "Russia and England will be at peace before the Colonel and Strux; I have no trust in any reconciliation of theirs.

For themselves, they could only repeat their pledges of mutual good-will.

Eleven days after the adventure with the chacmas, the

little troop, not far from the Zambesi Falls, arrived at a level plain several miles in extent, and perfectly adapted for the establishment of a base. On the edge of the plain rose a native village, composed of a few huts containing a small number of inhabitants, who kindly received the Europeans. Colonel Everest found the proximity of the natives very opportune, since the measurement of the base would occupy a month, and being without waggons, or any materials for an encampment, he would have had no resource but to pass the time in the open air, with no other shelter than that afforded by the foliage.

The astronomers took up their abode in the huts, which were quickly appropriated for the use of their new occupants. Their requirements were but small; their one thought was directed towards verifying their calculations by measuring the last side of their last triangle.

The astronomers at once proceeded to their work. The trestles and platinum rods were arranged with all the care that had been applied to the earliest base. Nothing was neglected; all the conditions of the atmosphere, and the variations of the thermometer, were taken into account, and the Commission, without flagging, brought every energy to bear upon their final operation.

The work, which lasted for five weeks, was completed on the 15th of May. When the lengths obtained had been estimated and reduced to the mean level of the sea at the temperature of 61° Fahrenheit, Palander and Emery presented to their colleagues the following numbers:—

	Toises.
New base actually measured	5075.25
The same base deduced trigonometrically from the entire series	5075.11
Difference between the calculation and the observation	.14

Thus there was only a difference of less than ⅙ of a toise that is to say, less than ten inches; yet the first base and the last were six hundred miles apart.

When the meridian of France was measured from Dunkirk to Perpignan, the difference between the base at Melun and that at Perpignan was eleven inches. The agreement obtained by the Anglo-Russian Commission was still more remarkable, and thus made the work accomplished in the deserts of Africa, amid dangers of every kind, more perfect than any previous geodetic operation.

The accuracy of this unprecedented result was greeted by the astronomers with repeated cheers.

According to Palander's reductions, the value of a degree in this part of the world was 57037 toises. This was within a toise, the same as was found by Lacaille at the Cape in 1752: thus, at the interval of a century, the French astronomer and the members of the Anglo-Russian Commission had arrived at almost exactly the same result.

Descending the Zambesi.—[Page 229.]

To deduce the value of the mètre, they would have to wait the issue of the operations which were to be afterwards undertaken in the northern hemisphere. This value was to be the $\frac{1}{10000000}$ of the quadrant of the terrestrial meridian. According to previous calculations, the quadrant, taking the depression of the earth into account, comprised 10,000,856 mètres, which brought the exact length of the mètre to .013074 of a toise, or 3 feet 0 inches 11.296 lines. Whether this was correct the subsequent labours of the Commission would have to decide.

* * * * *

The astronomers had now entirely finished their task, and it only remained for them to reach the mouth of the Zambesi, by following inversely the route afterwards taken by Dr. Livingstone in his second voyage from 1858 to 1864.

On the 25th of May, after a somewhat laborious journey across a country intersected with rivers, they reached the Victoria Falls. These fine cataracts fully justified their native name, which signifies "sounding smoke." Sheets of water a mile wide, crowned with a double rainbow, rushed from a height twice that of Niagara. Across the deep basalt chasm the enormous torrent produced a roar like peal after peal of thunder.

Below the cataract, where the river regained its calmness, the steamboat, which had arrived a fortnight previously by an inferior affluent of the Zambesi, awaited the astronomers, who soon took their places on board.

There were two to be left behind. Mokoum and the pioneer stood on the bank. In Mokoum the English were leaving, not only a devoted guide, but one whom they might call a friend. Sir John was especially sorry to part from him, and had offered to take him to Europe, and there entertain him as long as he pleased to remain. But Mokoum had previous engagements; in fact, he was to accompany Livingstone on the second voyage which the brave traveller was about to undertake up the Zambesi, and Mokoum was not a man to depart from his word. He was presented with a substantial recompense, and, what he prized still more, the kind assurances of regard of the Europeans, who acknowledged how much they owed to him. As the steamer left the shore to take the current in the middle of the river, Sir John's last gesture was to wave an adieu to his associate.

The descent of the great river, whose banks were dotted with numerous villages, was soon accomplished. The natives, regarding with superstitious admiration the smoking vessel as it moved by mysterious mechanism, made no attempt to obstruct its progress.

On the 15th of June the Colonel and his companions arrived at Quilimane, one of the principal towns at the mouth of the Zambesi. Their first thought was to ask for

Adieu to Mokoum.—[Page 230.]

The Natives regarded with superstitious admiration the smoking vessel.
[Page 230.]

news of the war. They found that it had not yet come to a termination, and that Sebastopol was still holding out against the allied armies. This was a disappointment to the Europeans, now so united in one scientific object; but they received the intelligence in silence, and prepared to start. An Austrian merchant-vessel, "La Novara," was just setting out for Suez; in that they resolved to take their passage.

Three days after, as they were on the point of embarking, the Colonel assembled his colleagues, and in a calm voice reminded them how in the last eighteen months they had together experienced many trials, and how they had been rewarded by accomplishing a work which would call forth the admiration of all scientific Europe. He could not refrain from giving expression to his trust that they would feel themselves bound in the common fellowship of a true alliance.

Strux bowed slightly, but did not interrupt the Colonel, who proceeded to deplore the tidings of the continuation of warfare. When he referred to the expected capitulation of Sebastopol, Strux indignantly rejected the possibility of such an event, which no union of France and England, he maintained, could ever effect.

There was, however, it was admitted on all hands, a propriety in the Russians and English submitting to the national status of hostility. The necessities of their position were thus clearly defined, and under these conditions they embarked in company on board "La Novara."

In a few days they arrived at Suez. At the moment of separation Emery grasped Zorn's hand, and said,—

"We are always friends, Michael!"

"Always and every where, William!" ejaculated Zorn; and with this sentiment of mutual devotion they parted.

The Commission was dissolved.

THE END.

Works of Jules Verne,
PUBLISHED BY
SCRIBNER, ARMSTRONG & CO.

THE COMPLETE AND AUTHORIZED EDITIONS.

CAUTION.

The public are cautioned against any editions of the works named below which do not bear the imprint of SCRIBNER, ARMSTRONG & CO. Any edition of these particular works published under other imprints are PIRATED, and cannot fail to be *inferior in every particular*. Editions bearing our imprint are issued under a direct arrangement with the French and English publishers of JULES VERNE, and are *authorized in text and complete in illustration*.

MERIDIANA:
THE ADVENTURES OF THREE ENGLISHMEN AND THREE RUSSIANS IN SOUTH AFRICA. By JULES VERNE. Translated from the French. With 48 illustrations. One vol. 12mo, cloth, gilt side and back. Price, 75 cents. The only edition authorized in text and complete in illustrations.

FROM THE EARTH TO THE MOON
IN 97 HOURS AND 20 MINUTES AND A TRIP AROUND IT. Eighty full-page illustrations, beautifully bound in cloth, black and gilt. Price, $3.00.

A JOURNEY to the CENTRE of the EARTH.
Translated from the French of JULES VERNE, author of "*From the Earth to the Moon Direct*," "*The Mysterious Island*," &c., &c. With fifty-two illustrations by Riou.

Popular edition, 20 *illustrations*, 75c. *Complete edition*, 53 *illustrations, on super-calendered paper, handsomely bound in cloth, black and gilt, beveled boards*, $3.00.

SCRIBNER, ARMSTRONG & CO.,
654 BROADWAY, NEW YORK

THE NOVEL OF THE YEAR.

ARTHUR BONNICASTLE,

By Dr. J. G. HOLLAND,

Author of "Bitter-Sweet," "Kathrina," "Titcomb's Letters," &c.

WITH TWELVE FULL-PAGE ILLUSTRATIONS BY MARY A. HALLOCK.

One Vol. 12mo, $1.75

ARTHUR BONNICASTLE is the most mature and finished prose work of its popular author. Autobiographic in form, it is partly so in material likewise; and while of thrilling interest as a story, it presents the ripe results of a life of earnest action and thought. The great lesson of the book is self-respect and self-reliance—the evil influence of dependence being exemplified in different characters and circumstances, by the youth of Arthur and the life of Peter Mullens. For character-drawing, purpose, pathos, style and savor of the soil, ARTHUR BONNICASTLE is remarkable among the novels of the time.

DR. HOLLAND'S WORKS.

Each in One Volume 12mo.

*BITTER-SWEET; a Poem . . $1 50	MISS GILBERT'S CAREER . . $2 00
*KATHRINA; a Poem . . . 1 50	BAY PATH 2 00
*LETTERS TO YOUNG PEOPLE, 1 50	THE MARBLE PROPHECY, and
GOLD FOIL, hammered from Popular Proverbs 1 75	other Poems 1 50
*LESSONS IN LIFE . . . 1 75	GARNERED SHEAVES, Complete Poetical Works, "Bitter-Sweet,"
*PLAIN TALKS on Familiar Subjects 1 75	"Kathrina," "Marble Prophecy," red line edition, beautifully illustrated. 4 00
LETTERS TO THE JONESES . 1 75	

* These six volumes are issued in Cabinet size (16mo), "Brightwood Edition," at the same prices as above.

Prices and Styles of the Different Editions

OF

FROUDE'S HISTORY OF ENGLAND.

The Chelsea Edition.

In half roan, gilt top, per set of twelve vols. 12mo... ....$21.00

Elegance and cheapness are combined in a remarkable degree in this edition. It takes its name from the place of Mr. Froude's residence in London, also famous as the home of Thomas Carlyle.

The Popular Edition.

In cloth, at the rate of $1.25 per volume. The set (12 vols.), in a neat box .$15.00
The Same, in half calf extra.. 36.00

This edition is printed from the same plates as the other editions, and on firm, white paper. It is, without exception, the cheapest set of books of its class ever issued in this country.

The Library Edition.

In twelve vols. crown 8vo, cloth............. ....$30.00
The Same, in half calf extra... 50.00

The Edition is printed on laid and tinted paper, at the Riverside Press, and is in every respect worthy a place in the most carefully selected library.

SHORT STUDIES ON GREAT SUBJECTS.

BY JAMES ANTHONY FROUDE, M.A.,
"*History of England*," "*The English in Ireland during the Eighteenth Century*," etc.

POPULAR EDITION. Two vols. 12mo, cloth, $1.50 per vol. The Set....$3.00
CHELSEA EDITION. Two vols. 12mo, half roan, gilt top, $2.00 per volume. Per Set... 4.00

The Complete Works of James Anthony Froude, M.A.

HISTORY OF ENGLAND AND SHORT STUDIES.
Fourteen vols., in a neat Box.

POPULAR EDITION...$18.00
CHELSEA EDITION... 25.00

The above works sent, post-paid, by the publishers, on receipt of the price.

SCRIBNER, ARMSTRONG & CO.,

654 BROADWAY, NEW YORK.

A NEW SERIES OF
The Illustrated Library of Wonders,

ENLARGED IN SIZE, IN A NEW STYLE OF BINDING, AND EDITED BY PROMINENT AMERICAN AUTHORS.

The extraordinary success of the ILLUSTRATED LIBRARY OF WONDERS has encouraged the publishers to still further efforts to increase the attractions and value of these admirable books. In the new series, which has just been commenced with THE WONDERS OF WATER, the size of the volumes is increased, the style of binding changed, and the successive volumes are edited by distinguished American authors and scientists.

The following volumes will introduce

THE SECOND SERIES.

WONDERS OF ELECTRICITY. Edited by Dr. J. W. ARMSTRONG, President of the State Normal School, Fredonia, N. Y. $1.50

WONDERS OF VEGETATION. (Over 40 Illustrations.) Edited by Prof. SCHELE DE VERE. $1.50

WONDERS OF WATER. (64 Illustrations.) Edited by Prof. SCHELE DE VERE.

WONDERS OF THE MOON. (With 50 Illustrations.) Edited, with additions, by Miss MARIA MITCHELL, of Vassar College, Poughkeepsie.

THE WONDERS OF SCULPTURE. From the French of LOUIS VIARDOT. With a chapter on American sculpture. With over sixty illustrations. $1.50

THE RED CLOTH, ORIGINAL STYLE OF THE FIRST SERIES OF

The Illustrated Library of Wonders

Reduced from $1.50 per volume to $1.25 per volume,
AND
From $30.00 to $25 per set of twenty volumes.

The First Series comprises:

	No. Illus.		No. Illus.
Wonderful Escapes	26	The Human Body	43
Bodily Strength and Skill	70	The Sublime in Nature	44
Balloon Ascents	30	Intelligence of Animals	54
Great Hunts	22	Thunder and Lightning	39
Egypt 3,300 Years ago	40	Bottom of the Sea	68
The Sun. By Guillemin	58	Italian Art	28
Wonders of Heat	93	European Art	11
Optical Wonders	71	Architecture	60
Wonders of Acoustics	110	Glass-Making	63
The Heavens	48	Wonders of Pompeii	22

Take Special Notice.—To get advantage of this reduction, be particular to specify **The Red Cloth Edition** in ordering. The price of sets of the first series, bound in half roan ($30.00, with rack), and that of single volumes of the second series ($1.50 per vol.), bound in green cloth, **remains unchanged.**

SUPPLEMENTARY VOLUMES TO THE FIRST SERIES.

MOUNTAIN ADVENTURES. (39 Illustrations.) Edited by Hon. J. T. HEADLEY.

WONDERS OF ENGRAVING. (: Illustrations.) Translated from the French of GEORGES DUPLESSIS.

☞ Any or all the volumes of the ILLUSTRATED LIBRARY OF WONDERS sent to any address, post or express charges paid, on receipt of the price.
A *Descriptive Catalogue* of the WONDER LIBRARY, *with specimen Illustrations,* *sent to any address, on application.*

SCRIBNER, ARMSTRONG & Co., 654 Broadway, N Y

A NEW AND VALUABLE SERIES
For Readers of all Ages and for the School & Family Library

THE ILLUSTRATED LIBRARY
OF
TRAVEL, EXPLORATION
AND ADVENTURE.
EDITED BY
BAYARD TAYLOR.

The extraordinary popularity of the ILLUSTRATED LIBRARY OF WONDERS (nearly one and a half million copies having been sold in this country and in France) is considered by the publishers a sufficient guarantee of the success of an ILLUSTRATED LIBRARY OF TRAVEL, EXPLORATION, AND ADVENTURE, embracing the same decidedly interesting and permanently valuable features. Upon this new enterprise the Publishers will bring to bear all their wide and constantly increasing resources. Neither pains nor expense will be spared in making their new Library not only one of the most elegantly and profusely illustrated works of the day, but at the same time one of the most graphic and fascinating in narrative and description.

Each volume will be complete in itself, and will contain, first, a brief preliminary sketch of the country to which it is devoted; next, such an outline of previous explorations as may be necessary to explain what has been achieved by later ones; and finally, a condensation of one or more of the most important narratives of recent travel, accompanied with illustrations of the scenery, architecture, and life of the races, drawn only from the most authentic sources. An occasional volume will also be introduced in the LIBRARY, detailing the exploits of individual adventurers. The entire series will thus furnish a clear, picturesque, and practical survey of our present knowledge of lands and races as supplied by the accounts of travellers and explorers. The LIBRARY will therefore be both entertaining and instructive to young as well as old, and the publishers intend to make it a necessity in every family of culture and in every private and public library in America. The name of BAYARD TAYLOR as editor is an assurance of the accuracy and high literary character of the publication.

NOW READY:

JAPAN,   **SIAM,**   **ARABIA,**
WILD MEN AND WILD BEASTS.
THE YELLOWSTONE.   SOUTH AFRICA.
CENTRAL ASIA.   CENTRAL AFRICA.

The volumes will be uniform in size (12mo), and in price, $1.50 each.
☞ *Catalogues, with specimen Illustrations, sent on application.*
SCRIBNER, ARMSTRONG & CO., 654 BROADWAY, N. Y.

The Works of George MacDonald

PUBLISHED BY

Scribner, Armstrong & Co.,

654 Broadway, New York.

THE HIDDEN LIFE

AND OTHER POEMS.

1 Vol., 12mo, $1.50.

This volume includes "The Hidden Life," MacDonald's well known poem "The Disciple," "The Gospel Women," "A Book of Sonnets," and the "Organ Songs," including the "Ode to Light,"—itself one of the most remarkable of modern poems.

WITHIN AND WITHOUT.

1 Vol., 12mo, $1.50.

This, which is the longest poem and one of the most important works of this popular author, is, in fact, a ***Thrilling Story in Verse.***

It deals in a graphic and masterly manner with the deepest human passion, is beautiful with imagination, and intensely interesting in plot. Macdonald is one of the most original and charming of living poets, and the many American readers of his prose works will be delighted at this opportunity of becoming acquainted with his poetry.

"All Mr. MacDonald's usual moral and spiritual subtlety and tendencies are these, and the story is full of the most lovely light."—*Contemporary Review.*

WILFRID CUMBERMEDE.

Author of "Alec. Forbes," "Annals of a Quiet Neighborhood," &c.

1 Vol., 12mo. Price $1.75. Cheap edition, paper, 75c., cloth, $1.25.

CRITICAL NOTICES.

"This book is full of intellectual wealth. It will teach us as many wise thoughts, and nurture as many noble feelings, as either 'Robert Falconer' or 'Alec. Forbes.'"—*British Quarterly Review.*

"It is simple, natural, pathetic, and playful by turns, interesting in plot and development of character, and written in such limpid English as it does one good to meet with."—*N. Y. Journal of Commerce.*

"The best story of him who is the best of living story-writers. It may be enjoyed almost in perfection by one who has not read the beginning, and who will never read the sequel; and it will remain in the memory like a beautiful song."—*N. Y. Independent.*

"Mr. Macdonald's writing are beautiful in style, powerful in description, pathetic and pure in their design."—*Christian Intelligencer.*

☞ *These works sent, post paid, upon receipt of the price.*

The Erckmann-Chatrian Novels

THE CONSCRIPT: *A Tale of the French War of 1813.* With four full-page Illustrations. One vol. 12mo. Price, in paper, 75 cents; cloth, $1.25.

From the Cincinnati Daily Commercial.

"It is hardly fiction,—it is history in the guise of fiction, and that part of history which historians hardly write, concerning the disaster, the ruin, the sickness, the poverty, and the utter misery and suffering which war brings upon the people."

WATERLOO: *A Story of the Hundred Days.* Being a Sequel to "*The Conscript.*" With four full-page Illustrations. One vol. 12mo. Price, in paper, 75 cents; cloth, $1.25.

From the New York Daily Herald.

"Written in that charming style of simplicity which has made the ERCKMANN-CHATRIAN works popular in every language in which they have been published."

THE BLOCKADE OF PHALSBURG. An Episode of the Fall of the First French Empire. With four full-page Illustrations and a Portrait of the authors. One vol. 12mo. Price, in paper, 75 cents; cloth, $1.25.

From the Philadelphia Daily Inquirer.

"Not only are they interesting historically, but intrinsically a pleasant, well-constructed plot, serving in each case to connect the great events which they so graphically treat, and the style being as vigorous and charming as it is pure and refreshing."

INVASION OF FRANCE IN 1814. With the Night March past Phalsburg. With a Memoir of the Authors. With four full-page Illustrations. One vol. 12mo. Price, in paper, 75 cents; cloth, $1.25.

From the New York Evening Mail.

"All their novels are noted for the same admirable qualities,—simple and effective realism of plot, incident, and language, and a disclosure of the horrid individual aspects of war. They are absolutely perfect of their kind."

MADAME THERESE; *or, The Volunteers '92.* With four full-page Illustrations. One vol. 12mo. Price, in paper, 75 cents; cloth, $1.25.

From the Boston Commonwealth.

"It is a boy's story—that is, supposed to be written by a boy—and has all the freshness, the unconscious simplicity and *naïveté* which the imagined authorship should imply; while nothing more graphic, more clearly and vividly pictorial, has been brought before the public for many a day."

Any or all of the above volumes sent, post-paid, upon receipt of the price by the publishers.

SCRIBNER, ARMSTRONG & CO.,

(Successors to CHARLES SCRIBNER & Co.),

654 Broadway, New York.

"The very best, the most sensible, the most practical, the most honest book on this matter of getting up good dinners, and living in a decent Christian way, that has yet found its way into our household."—*Watchman and Reflector.*

COMMON SENSE
In the Household.
A MANUAL OF PRACTICAL HOUSEWIFERY,
By MARION HARLAND,
Author of "Alone," "Hidden Path," "Nemesis," &c., &c.

One vol. 12mo, cloth. Price...................$1 75

SEE WHAT THE CRITICS, AND PRACTICAL HOUSEKEEPERS, say of it:

" And now we have from another popular novelist a cookery book, whereof our housekeeper (this literary recorder is not a bachelor) speaks most enthusiastically. She says that simplicity and clearness of expression, accuracy of detail, a regard to economy or material, and certainty of good results, are requisites in a useful receipt-book for the kitchen, and Marion Harland has comprehended all these. That she has by experience proved the unsatisfactoriness of housekeepers' helps in general is shown by the arrangement of her book. She has appended a star to such recipes as, after having tried them herself, she can recommend as safe and generally simple. Such a directory will be a great help to one who goes to the book for aid in preparing a pleasant and savory meal without much experience in cooking. The language is so simple, and the directions so plain, that a reasonably intelligent cook might avail herself of it to vary her manner of preparing even ordinary dishes. The introduction to the book should be printed as a tract and put in every house. The simple advice for the management of servants, the general directions at the head of each department of cooking, and the excellent pages on the sick-room, make as complete an aid to housekeepers as can well be desired."—*Harper's Monthly.*

" In the hands of the author, whose name is well known in another department of literature, the subject has been treated with thoroughness and skill, showing that a little common sense may be as successful in the concoction of a toothsome viand as in the composition of a romance."—*N. Y. Daily Tribune.*

" It inspires us with a great respect for the housewifery of a literary lady, and we cannot err in predicting for it a wide popularity."—*N. Y. Evening Post.*

" Unites the merits of a trustworthy receipt-book with the freshness of a familiar talk on household affairs."—*Albany Evening Journal.*

" The directions are clear, practical, and so good in their way that the only wonder is, how any one head could hold so many pots, kettles, and pans, and such a world of gastronomic good things."—*Hearth and Home.*

" The recipes are clearly expressed, easy to follow, and not at all expensive. The suggestions about household affairs are *chic.* On a test comparison with three other American cook-books, it comes out ahead upon every count. Beyond this *experto crede* nothing more need be said."—*Christian Union.*

Copies sent, post-paid, on receipt of the price, by

SCRIBNER, ARMSTRONG & CO.,
654 Broadway, New York

A CAPITAL STORY
— BY —
JULES VERNE,
Author of "A Journey to the Centre of the Earth."

FROM THE EARTH TO THE MOON DIRECT

In 97 Hours, 20 Minutes,
AND A TRIP AROUND IT.

EIGHTY FULL-PAGE ILLUSTRATIONS.

One vol., 12mo, bevelled boards, $3.00.

This is one of the most stirring and exciting of Jules Verne's famous and popular stories. Three adventurers take passage for the moon in a hollow, conical shell, weighing 20,000 lbs., and projected from a cannon 900 feet long by the explosion of 400,000 lbs. of gun-cotton. The tremendous results of this explosion; the rush through space of the shell and its passengers; the extent to which they were able to conquer the laws of gravitation, and the results of their extraordinary exploit, make up as thrilling a series of adventures as the fancy of this very imaginative French author is capable of painting. Numerous facts in philosophy, astronomy, and other sciences, are woven into the story, which is spiced with not a little good-humored satire upon American peculiarities, for the scene of the narrative is laid to a great extent in the United States.

☞ *Sent post-paid on receipt of price, by the Publishers,*

SCRIBNER, ARMSTRONG & CO.,
654 Broadway, New York.

"Infinite Riches in a Little Room."—*Marlowe.*

THE
BRIC-A-BRAC SERIES,

Personal reminiscences of famous poets, novelists, wits and humorists, artists, actors, musicians, and the like.

Edited by RICHARD HENRY STODDARD.

NOW READY THE INITIAL VOLUME:

Personal Reminiscences.

CHORLEY, PLANCHE, and YOUNG.

One volume, square 12mo, beautifully bound in extra cloth, black and gilt, price $1.50.

Seldom has so much amusement been crowded between a single set of not large covers as may be found in the first volume of the BRIC-A-BRAC SERIES. Owing to Mr. Stoddard's careful and judicious editing, we have here in a nutshell all the best things from the three recently issued books of biography and reminiscence, by or about Chorley, the Athenæum's musical critic, Planche, the popular dramatist, and Young the eminent actor. The pages fairly brim with descriptions, quips and anecdotes anent famous philosophers, poets, wits, actors, singers, politicians—men and women now out of the world in which they were once so busy and conspicuous. It would require the repetition of the entire index to give a full idea of the number of interesting people discussed and described here. Napoleon III., with the diamond eagle, just before he sported the famous real one at Boulogne; George III., with his querulous ways; delightful Malibran; our own Hawthorne; Byron the reckless; Count D'Orsay, still princely in his poverty; Thackeray the rollicksome; Bulwer, Kean, Lady Blessington, Tom Hood, and scores of others, for whose names even there is not room.

CRITICAL NOTICES.

"No more refreshing volumes could be carried into the country or to the sea-shore, to fill up the niches of time which intervene between the pleasures of the summer holidays. *Boston Post.*

"If this first volume is a fair specimen of his [the editor's] judgment and skill, the series will prove first-class and popular, among lovers of pure literature."—*Providence Press.*

"A well-dressed book, in a light May suit, with a spring overcoat.... None more entertaining for the odd hours of leisure, and especially for the after-dinner breathing-time of day has for a long time been published.... We commend the book to the summer tourist who can be content with anything better than a novel, and will condescend to be amused."—*Worcester Gazette.*

"Mr. Stoddard's work appears to be done well-nigh perfectly. There is not a dull page in the book."—*N. Y. Evening Post.*

www.ingramcontent.com/pod-product-compliance
Lightning Source LLC
Chambersburg PA
CBHW030319240426
43673CB00040B/1213